THROUGH THE WORDS OF 400 INTERNATIONAL
RESEARCH PARTICIPANTS

Have The Numbers Gone Nuts?

The Research Guide to Neurodiverse
(Autistic-Neurotypical) Relationships

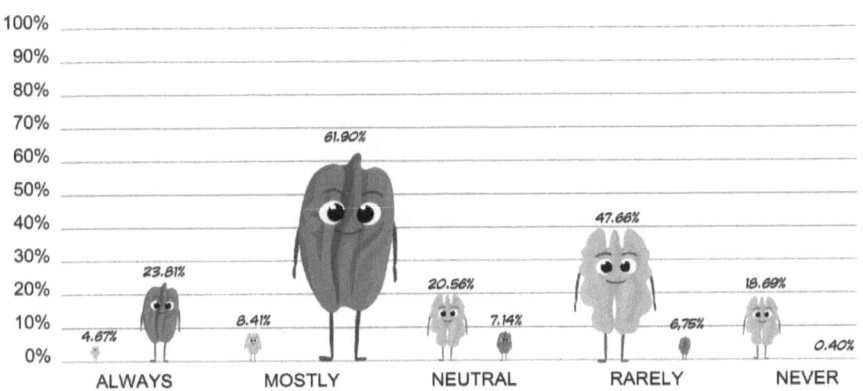

SI 13
I find it easy to communicate what I am feeling

Dr Bronwyn Maree Wilson
Foreword by Professor Tony Attwood

First published by Ultimate World Publishing 2025
Copyright © 2025 Dr Bronwyn Wilson

ISBN

Paperback: 978-1-923425-11-8
Ebook: 978-1-923425-12-5

Dr Bronwyn Wilson has asserted her rights under the Copyright, Designs and Patents Act 1988 to be identified as the author of this work. The information in this book is based on the author's experiences and opinions. The publisher specifically disclaims responsibility for any adverse consequences which may result from use of the information contained herein. Permission to use information has been sought by the author. Any breaches will be rectified in further editions of the book.

All rights reserved. No part of this publication may be reproduced, stored in or introduced into a retrieval system, or transmitted in any form, or by any means (electronic, mechanical, photocopying, recording or otherwise) without the prior written permission of the author. Any person who does any unauthorised act in relation to this publication may be liable to criminal prosecution and civil claims for damages. Enquiries should be made through the publisher.

Cover design: Ultimate World Publishing
Layout and typesetting: Ultimate World Publishing
Editor: Marinda Wilkinson

Ultimate World Publishing
Diamond Creek,
Victoria Australia 3089
www.writeabook.com.au

Dedication

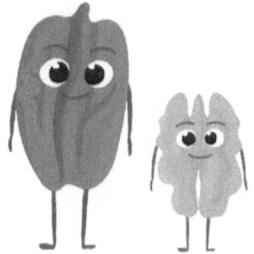

This book is dedicated to my husband Michael, who inspired me to return to further studies and continues to support and encourage me to devote time and attention to my research and writing.

I would also like to dedicate this book to my immediate and extended family members, who along with numerous friends, bestowed on me substantial understanding of the impacts of autism spectrum conditions on and within relationships.

Contents

DEDICATION	iii
FOREWORD	xi
INTRODUCTION	1
SHAKING OFF THE PAST	1
Never Going There Again!	2
A New Story	3
Three From Two	6
1. MARCHING TO DIFFERENT DRUMS	11
Contrasting Components	13
Staggering Shortcomings	15
Relationship Realities	17
Participation Particulars	20
Evidential Elements	22
2. AN EXPRESSIVE DIVIDE	27
A Remarkable Finding	28

Have The Numbers Gone Nuts?

The Formula	30
The Emotional Divide	31
The Personal Divide	40
The Meaningful Divide	43
A Collision of More with Less	50
3. A STRANGLEHOLD	**57**
Anxiety's Assault	59
Anxiety's Hold	62
4. A NEEDS DIVIDE	**65**
Together Apart	66
The Need for Solitude's Calmative Effect	72
Left Wanting	81
Unravelling Households	91
5. IRRECONCILABLE DIFFERENCES	**101**
Perceptions and Detections	102
An Awareness Divide	105
Hijacked by Roadblocks	111
6. A DISTINCTIVE DYNAMIC	**117**
Striving for a Remedy	119
Seeking Responses	128
Struggling to Hold Discussions	131
Surviving Conflict	133
7. SELF-PROTECTIVE TRIGGERS	**139**
Talking Tensions	141
Talking More or Less	145
Hit and Miss	147
8. COMPETITIVE LOOPS	**151**
A Pervasive Tug-of-War	153

Contents

Detachment Dangers	155
Surviving the Discord	157
9. DISASTROUS DEVELOPMENTS	**169**
At Cross Purposes	170
An Arising Burden	173
10. COMPLICATED ADDITIONS	**177**
Cycles Within Cycles	178
Devastating Judgements	189
A Disastrous Dynamic	192
11. VARIOUS AFTERMATHS	**201**
Thriving	202
Surviving	206
Deteriorating	209
12. DEFINING PATTERNS	**215**
The Numbers Narrative	216
Constructive Considerations	222
Drawing Conclusions	225
SPEAKER BIO	**231**
ABOUT THE AUTHOR	**233**
ACKNOWLEDGEMENTS	**235**
REFERENCES	**237**

And we know [with great confidence]

that God [who is deeply concerned about us]

causes all things to work together

[as a plan] for good for those who love God,

to those who are called according to His plan and purpose.

Romans 8:28, Amplified Bible

Foreword

I have thoroughly enjoyed reading the first two books in the 'Going Nuts' series and greatly appreciated the insights into neurodiverse relationships. We now have Book Three, which includes data that will be valuable for relationship counsellors, neurodiverse couples and families, as well as academics.

My clinical experience and recent research confirm that conventional relationship counselling is perceived as having a positive effect by only 29% of neurodiverse couples and perceived as unhelpful in 44% of neurodiverse couples (Attwood and Aston, 2025; Smith et al., 2021).

Those relationship counsellors who had experience and training in autism were more likely to be rated positively. This book provides the data needed for relationship counsellors to understand the issues experienced by neurodiverse couples

Have The Numbers Gone Nuts?

and adapt their counselling to accommodate the effects of autism in a relationship, as described throughout the series.

Neurodiverse couples will appreciate the validation of their thoughts, feelings and experiences and resonate with the quotations and descriptions of everyday relationship experiences. I have found that autistic individuals have become engrossed in the series, as reading is often their preferred way of absorbing new information rather than conversation with a partner or relationship counsellor.

Academics and counselling courses will recognise the value of data and data analysis, and the series will encourage further research, the development and application of theoretical models, and enhance professional training for counsellors, psychologists and psychiatrists.

Professor Tony Attwood

Attwood and Aston (2025) *Relationship Counselling with Autistic Neurodiverse Couples*, London, Jessica Kingsley Publishers

Smith, R., Netto, J., Gribble, N. C., & Falkmer, M. (2021). 'At the end of the day, it's love': an exploration of relationships in neurodiverse couples. *Journal of Autism and Developmental Disorders, 51*, 3311-3321.

Introduction

Shaking Off the Past

'Failure is the opportunity to
begin again more intelligently.'
Henry Ford

Have The Numbers Gone Nuts?

Never Going There Again!

My high school years became anything but enjoyable after a few classmates had decided to target me. Their relentless taunts became a daily battle and as time went on, the weight of their constant insults became unbearable. In a moment of desperation, I decided to drop out of high school.

My parents agreed that I could leave school if I found a job. So that's what I did. I took the first job that came along and that was that. The headmaster could not change my mind. He said that I would come to regret my decision, but my mind was made up. I left two months before the end of the school year with the thought in my head, 'I am never going back to school ever again!'

Well, they do say, never say never. Many years later, when finding myself in the position of needing to provide for teenage children, and with obsolete skills and no other qualifications to speak of, back to school I went. With some trepidation, but much determination, I enrolled in a college course.

The challenge of returning to the origin of much torment and humiliation soon became a source of fulfilment and satisfaction. My passion for learning was rekindled. I rediscovered a love of reading and writing. Despite the years away from formal education, I found that I was excelling academically. As my confidence grew, so did my academic ambitions. I decided to go on to university and complete a teaching degree.

A few years later, with a Bachelor of Education under my belt, I was ready to embark on a new chapter: teaching. Although teaching brought much enjoyment and satisfaction, after some years, things took an unexpected turn. My teaching career had awakened an understanding of the autism spectrum with a growing realisation that many of my immediate and extended family members were most probably on the autism spectrum. Armed with a desire to know more, I said goodbye to teaching and pivoted my career towards research – and back to school I went, again.

Entering teaching had activated what leaving teaching had crystallised. Born from years of reflecting on the details of challenging interactions, both inside and outside of the classroom environment, my research focus was on communication in neurodiverse relationships, that is relationships that include people with an autism spectrum condition (ASC) and non-autistic people (considered neurotypical, NT).

A New Story

In the years that followed, most of my days were filled with talking and chatting with people in neurodiverse relationships and sending out surveys. Long hours were spent at the computer transcribing interviews, analysing survey data and poring over the patterns and similarities that were emerging in the data. After a painstaking evaluation of the developing results, I stumbled upon a pattern in the data that showed commonalities between people in neurodiverse relationships regardless of where they were from, or to what culture they belonged.

Consulting with my supervisors, we realised I had uncovered a previously unknown communication phenomenon

Have The Numbers Gone Nuts?

that was found to be common across all the neurodiverse relationships I had studied. In addition, the wide range of national and international participants demonstrated a cross-cultural similarity of responses. I had discovered that a pairing of the two different communication needs and styles between ASC and NT people resulted in a number of identifiably distinguishing communication complications which formed into a distinctive cycle between them. Since the cycle's central feature was a dependency on prompting, it was decided a suitable label was The Prompt Dependency Cycle (see Figure 12.1 at the back of the book).

Prompting is a well-established procedure to facilitate learning and is commonly used with children on the spectrum to compensate for the challenges related to independent functioning and motivation (Swerdan & Rosales, 2017). However, the cues and prompting strategies aimed at managing these difficulties can result in an over-reliance on adult support and development of a dependency on the prompts (Milley & Machalicek, 2012). In addition, prompt dependency can contribute to learned helplessness and the belief that one's own behaviour does not control outcomes or results (Sternberg & Williams, 2010).

My research uncovered that people with autism can continue to require this type of support throughout their lifetime. Therefore, the resulting dependency on the supporting prompts of others can also be lifelong, which may also result in the ongoing need to manage feelings of helplessness.

It was discovered that upon entering a romantic relationship, adults on the spectrum can develop a dependency on the prompts of their significant others as a result of the very different needs of each in these relationships to share in emotional reciprocal interaction – that is, the need to avoid reciprocal interaction (ASC), contrasted with the need to have reciprocal interaction (NT). In other words, when these different communication needs and abilities converge with a tendency towards prompt dependency and are accompanied by prompting, the blend of these behaviours can form into an ongoing communication cycle. The need for reciprocal emotional connectedness (NT) and the need to avoid reciprocal emotional connectedness (ASC) were the common threads that kept prompting and prompt dependency and/or prompt avoidance cycling between people in these relationships. Whether the relationship was romantic, parent-child or between siblings, the association between different needs, expectancies and capabilities of autistic and NT individuals were the catalyst to the formation of the prompt dependency cycle in these relationships.

Due to the very different needs and abilities between NT and ASC people, this prompt dependency cycle was found to function in a similar way across all neurodiverse relationships studied. Additionally, it was noticed that this cycle gave rise to a specific style of unconventionality across all relationships studied. Since neurodiverse relationships are widespread, the discovery of this cycle can be no mere anomaly, but a revelation, a piece of the puzzle of these relationships that needs to be recognised. Yet, general lack of awareness surrounding these types of relationships perpetuates misunderstanding and isolation. In order to bring this rather common, yet hidden, reality of these relationships out into the open, further investigation needs to take place. It is my desire that my research and the data this book contains will open the floodgates, and that the information held within this series of books will inspire many researchers to take up the challenge to further study neurodiverse relationships.

So, after uncovering this cycle through a choice made many years ago to go back to school, I found that dropping out of high school had not been the end of my story. It was, instead, one of the opening chapters. I realised that the pursuit of knowledge knows no age or background. A passion for helping others can overcome shadows of the past and can lead to embracing a brighter future. In the end, my triumph was not just in obtaining a PhD, but in turning a painful past into a source of strength and resilience that will not only benefit myself, but also those who walk a similar path.

Three From Two

Have The Numbers Gone Nuts? is the last book in the three-book series that describes the results of two research studies on communication within neurodiverse relationships, that is, relationships in which at least one person is on the autism spectrum. The two studies extended over a period of eight years with the investigation of the second study based on the findings from the first. The broad focus of both studies was on adults with an autism spectrum condition (ASC) and communication in their close relationships. Particular attention was devoted to the characteristics of prompt dependency and how it forms into a communication cycle between those in neurodiverse relationships.

Four hundred research participants describe the 'craziness' and yet, also 'not craziness' of living on the inside of a different kind of relationship. A relationship that looks quite 'normal' on the outside but is anything but normal on the inside. Conveyed from the distinct position of each group of participants, the three-book series is designed to be an informative journey behind the closed doors of neurodiverse relationships. The words and perspectives of both adults with ASC and neurotypical adults are interwoven together throughout all three books as we proceed through the different topics under investigation in each book.

The first book in the series provided an overview of neurodiverse relationships, while also describing how the two behaviours of prompting and prompt dependency converge into a communication cycle. The underlying dynamics of the prompt dependency cycle was illustrated by revealing how the elements of the cycle interacted within a complex system of competing needs, roles, expectations and problem-solving behaviours. It described all the internal relational aspects that are a consequence of this communication system and how it impacts on each in these relationships. Also provided were identifiable actions to consider implementing to encourage the potential for those in neurodiverse relationships to thrive.

The second book in the series built on the information contained in the first. Through the participants' narratives, we discovered the different approaches to life between people on the autism spectrum and neurotypical people and how their differences affect their relationships. Also explored was what takes place when they reach out for comfort, validation, encouragement and support from family, friends and professionals. Since many clinicians and counsellors went through their education at a time when the autism spectrum was relatively unknown, the second book was intended as a resource to gain an understanding of the difference between neurodiverse relationships and typical relationships. Intended to enhance awareness of these matters, the second book shared the challenges that the participants faced when involved in clinical settings and their viewpoints about the different approaches that they need from professionals.

This third book of the *Have They Gone Nuts* series further describes the underlying dynamics of the prompt dependency cycle while also revealing the research data derived from the studies. The data will be crucial for policy makers, practitioners and other stakeholders to inform program improvement and future program development. Academics should also consider the data gained from this study in crafting new (or refining existing) research, interventions and programs for people in neurodiverse relationships as it directly incorporates their voices.

So, who are the research participants? Firstly, a research Master of Special Education, a small-scale study of nine couples was completed at Griffith University, Brisbane, Australia in 2013. The nine couples all comprised one person who would previously have been identified with Asperger's Syndrome (either diagnosed or self-diagnosed) and one NT person. The Doctor of Philosophy research, a larger international study, began two years later and was completed at Edith Cowan University, Perth, Australia in 2020. Included were partners, parents, adult siblings and adult children involved in neurodiverse relationships; specifically, relationships that include people with ASC and neurotypical people. Participants were from Australia, the United Kingdom and the United States of America, as well as, Africa, Asia, Canada, Europe, the Middle East and New Zealand. To protect anonymity, survey participants remained anonymous, and all interview participants were assigned a pseudonym.

The *Have They Gone Nuts* series is intended to be used as a resource for neurodiverse families and couples, anyone who suspects that they may be in a neurodiverse relationship, family and friends of people in neurodiverse relationships, counsellors, therapists and service providers who work with the neurodiverse population, those who research neurodiverse relationships and anyone who wants to increase their understanding of neurodiverse families and couples. It is hoped that by reading the testimonies of the 400 participants involved in the two studies, it will not only promote greater understanding of this population, but it will also assist in bridging the knowledge gap that currently exists between many service providers and the community in general, about the unique relationship experiences of neurodiverse families and couples.

1

Marching to Different Drums

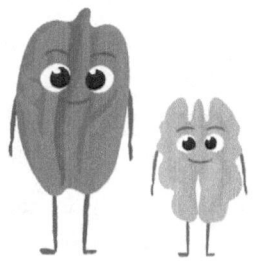

'If a man does not keep pace with his companions, perhaps it is because he hears a different drummer. Let him step to the music which he hears, however measured or far away.'
Henry David Thoreau

Have The Numbers Gone Nuts?

People on the autism spectrum see the world differently, process information in a unique way, and sometimes feel overwhelmed by the world around them. Often, they possess an extraordinary memory and an ability to focus intensely on things that fascinate them. These distinctions are due to differences in brain wiring, which has a strong genetic component, but environmental factors can also contribute (Amaral, 2017).

Although autism is categorised as a single syndrome, it can be understood as a spectrum of conditions that are primarily biological, rather than behavioural, in nature (Casanova & Casanova, 2019). Despite this, diagnosis is usually centred on behaviour. Autism is characterised by early-onset and persistent difficulties with reciprocal social communication and interactions as well as restricted, repetitive patterns of behaviour, interests or activities. Autism is a difference in brain wiring that influences how the brain processes information (Braden et al., 2017). With lifelong effects due to a lower grey matter volume in the regions of the brain that process social signals, when compared to non-autistic people (Sato et al., 2017), these differences influence how social information is processed and how they interact with the world around them.

Up until recently, autism diagnoses were divided into categories like autistic disorder (AD), Asperger's syndrome (AS) and pervasive developmental disorder not otherwise specified (PDD-NOS) (Grzadzinski et al., 2013). However, in 2013, with the release of the *DSM-5*, these divisions were combined into a single diagnosis: autism spectrum disorder (ASD). This change was made to simplify understanding of autism and streamline the diagnostic process. However, there's been a lot of debate, especially about including Asperger's syndrome in this broader category. Although Asperger's syndrome is no longer a separate diagnosis, many people still use the term. Lately, the phrase 'autism spectrum condition' (ASC) has gained popularity because some feel the word 'disorder' is outdated and carries negative connotations. While the *DSM-5* continues to use 'disorder', some experts believe it's time to reconsider how we label these conditions (Baron-Cohen, 2015).

Additionally, a study by the Centres for Disease Control (CDC) found that most autistic people (59%) do not have an intellectual disability (Maenner et al., 2020). Consistent with these findings, my research focuses on the communication styles of people with autism spectrum conditions (ASC) who have more subtle challenges. This includes individuals who might have previously been diagnosed with Asperger's syndrome or those without an accompanying intellectual disability.

Contrasting Components

Autism spectrum conditions (ASC) are mainly characterised by challenges in social interactions and social functioning (Fletcher-Watson et al., 2013; White et al., 2015). Social interaction involves using both verbal and non-verbal cues such as eye contact, speech, gestures, tone of voice and facial expressions, to connect with others. For most people, social interaction comes naturally, allowing them to understand others' feelings and intentions just by observing and interacting. As Caruana et al. (2017) describe, social interaction is a back-and-forth process, as in, my behaviour influences yours, and yours affects mine. However, for people with ASC, coordinating attention with someone else to engage in this give-and-take of social interaction can be particularly difficult.

Social functioning refers to typical behaviour in social situations. It involves the ability to start, maintain and coordinate mutual activities and relationships with others and difficulties with these aspects are a defining feature of autism spectrum conditions (Bishop-Fitzpatrick et al., 2017). Social functioning is supported by social development and cognition which involves learning how to think about oneself and others, including understanding thoughts, desires and emotions.

Research shows that neurotypical people, often behave and think differently from those on the autism spectrum (Novacek et al., 2016). The term 'neurotypical' (NT) was originally used by the autistic community to describe people without such conditions and has since been widely adopted by both the neurodiversity movement and the scientific community to refer to the general population.

Compared to people with ASC, NT individuals tend to need more social interaction, especially in close relationships (Moreno et al., 2012). Regular, deep conversations help them feel connected and increase their sense of wellbeing (Brown et al., 2007; Webster et al., 2009). Given that social skills come naturally to them, NT people do not experience the same challenges in understanding emotions or engaging in social interactions as those with autism do. For NT individuals, being able to connect emotionally, express love, and give and receive support through social interactions is key to their relationships.

Marching to Different Drums

When relationships involve both autistic and neurotypical people, the differences between them can create unique dynamics that do not always follow the typical pattern of interaction. Despite these differences, research has found that strong social interaction and functioning abilities are linked to a better quality of life for everyone (Addabbo et al., 2016; Tobin et al., 2014). Yet it seems that autistic and neurotypical people often operate on different wavelengths. It can be said that each is hearing a different drummer and this difference shapes how each experiences relationships and social connections.

Staggering Shortcomings

Although the formal history of autism is less than a century old, it has existed long before it had a name. Autism spectrum conditions have been documented across cultures and throughout history (Deisinger, 2011). For example, a 13th-century book describes the behaviour of a monk that suggests he may have been on the spectrum. It's also believed that several historical figures, including Albert Einstein, Amadeus Mozart, Isaac Newton, Charles Darwin and Michelangelo, may have had characteristics of autism (Elder & Thomas, 2006; James, 2005).

What we now know is that people on the autism spectrum have unique differences compared to neurotypical people due to genetic factors and distinct brain wiring, especially in areas related to social behaviour. Many studies such as those by Donovan & Basson (2017), O'Hearn and Lynn (2023) and Sato et al. (2017) highlight some of these distinct brain differences. However, as Pellicano et al. (2014) points out, most of the funding for autism research has been directed toward basic science, like studying genetics and neural systems, rather than focusing on the everyday experiences of autistic individuals. In addition, much of this research tends to focus on children, leaving a significant gap in understanding the lives of autistic adults (Perkins & Berkman, 2012). This lack of attention has resulted in a poor understanding of what life is like for most autistic adults (Sachdeva & Jones, 2018).

Because research influences what the public knows, this limited exploration into adult autism means very little is known about how autistic adults live, their social involvement, or their mental and physical health (Howlin & Magiati, 2017). The shortage of studies means that most people do not have a clear picture of how autism manifests in adults, leading to widespread myths and misconceptions. Since autism exists on a spectrum, there's a wide range of how it manifests (Marica, 2018) and many autistic adults fly under the radar because their traits are less noticeable. However, that does not make them any less autistic, just less recognised. This hidden nature of autism means that often only those directly affected truly understand the differences and difficulties.

These misunderstandings are particularly common when it comes to people who might have once been diagnosed with Asperger's syndrome or those who remain undiagnosed or misdiagnosed. According to Lai and Baron-Cohen (2015), individuals with more obvious symptoms, like severe social withdrawal or developmental delays, are often diagnosed early. However, those with subtler traits, such as those who might have been identified with Asperger's in the past, are often diagnosed later, if at all. It's also not widely recognised that autism is a lifelong condition, not something you grow out of (Marica, 2018). Autistic adults may learn to manage or mask their traits as they age, but that does not mean they are any less autistic or that they no longer face challenges. Additionally, despite its long history, many people still do not realise that autism is primarily genetic, and if a child is diagnosed, it's likely that one or both parents may be on the spectrum too. Unfortunately, many of these topics are rarely discussed or researched openly.

Due to this widespread lack of understanding, many misconceptions about autistic adults persist. Media portrayals, such as those in *Rain Man*, *The Big Bang Theory* or *The Good Doctor*, often create the false impression that all autistic individuals either have extraordinary abilities, serious disabilities or are quirky loners, with no in-between (Marica, 2018). We need more representation of the diverse range of autistic individuals in the media, more research about everyday experiences of autistic individuals and greater efforts to raise awareness of autism in adulthood. John et al. (2018) suggest that identifying and challenging myths about autism could help create educational programs to improve public understanding.

Relationship Realities

Although we now know that autistic adults often have a similar interest in close relationships as neurotypical adults (Hancock et al., 2019; Smith et al., 2020; Yew et al., 2023; Yew et al., 2021), there's still much that we do not know about what happens in relationships where one or both partners are neurodiverse. This gap in research leaves both communities and professionals lacking insight into the specific needs of autistic adults, their partners and their families. Until studies increase on how relationships work between autistic and neurotypical people, we will lack the understanding of the unique challenges these families face which limits the practical advice that can be offered to autistic adults and those around them.

What is known is that families and relationships that involve autistic people are distinct. A study by Cridland et al. (2014) discovered that having a family member on the autism spectrum results in a variety of specific challenges for all members of the family, including 'accommodation of inflexible daily routines, lack of spontaneity, management of unique intolerances and sudden mood changes, and being mediators in social interactions' (p. 214). While these struggles are well-known in families with autistic children, the larger focus on children or medical aspects of autism (Pellicano et al., 2014), has meant there is little knowledge of how these challenges play out in the daily lives of adults and their relationships.

Like all relationships, neurodiverse relationships experience challenges, but they tend to be different in nature. The differences in how autistic and neurotypical brains are wired create a distinct type of relationship, whether or not autism is acknowledged. The needs and abilities of each person can sometimes clash, making these relationships hard to compare to conventional ones. It's like having two people marching to their own beats, but trying to walk in step with each other. As a result, neurodiverse couples often face relationship patterns that are different from what most people experience.

Managing the contrasts that result from the pairing of different neurologies can be difficult when understanding that autism underpins these contrasts. However, if autism is unknown, disregarded or denied, managing the resulting contrasts can be even more difficult. Whether or not autism is recognised as a feature of the relationship, the resulting incompatibilities that develop between the two types of people are usually only seen behind closed doors. From the outside, these relationships do not look much different to regular relationships.

Likewise, the camouflaging behaviours that many people on the autism spectrum perform can affect relationships. As described in Books 1 and 2, most people on the autism spectrum become adept at camouflaging their autism in public (Mandy, 2019). As Pearson and Rose (2021) explain, 'masking' or camouflaging is a response to the negative stereotypes and stigma around autism. While it helps people appear more socially acceptable, it can make life more difficult in the long run. It affects mental health (Cage & Troxell-Whitman, 2020) and makes it hard for autistic adults to accept their true selves after years of pretending to be someone they are not.

Masking also adds stress to relationships. At home, where it feels safe, autistic adults often let their guard down, revealing their true behaviours, which can be very different from how they act in public. This shift can create a hidden divide between how things are inside the home and outside of it, making it harder for their partners and family members to navigate the relationship.

Since these dynamics are largely invisible to the outside world, people in neurodiverse relationships often face challenges they have little knowledge of how to manage. Unfortunately, most clinicians, counsellors and healthcare professionals went through their education at a time when autism was mainly unknown, so they have little to no experience in recognising autism in adults and often do not know how to work with neurodiverse couples. This means that therapists often use strategies that do not work in the context of these relationships (Anon, 2020; Lipinski et al., 2021).

Some studies, such as the work of Arad (2020); Arad et al. (2022); Bostock-Ling (2017); Bostock-Ling et al. (2012); Hancock et al. (2019); Lau and Peterson (2011); Lewis (2017); Lorant (2011); Millar-Powell and Warburton (2020); Rench (2014); Rossetti (2020); Smith et al. (2020); Yew et al. (2023); Yew et al. (2021), together with my studies, have begun to turn the tide. However, much of the results of these studies are yet to filter through to the general population. Accordingly, we need many more studies conducted on these mainly unfamiliar types of relationships.

Participation Particulars

In my first study, a total of 9 couples were interviewed. In the second study, 21 people participated in a pilot study which was used to obtain participant feedback before designing the main part of the study. The second study used a mixed methods approach which allowed for the collection and analysis of quantitative (survey) and qualitative (interview) data. A total of 360 people completed the survey phase. One participant completed two surveys based on two different relationships. A total of 44 people also completed the interview phase of the study. Participants were asked to select their gender; male, female or other, recognising that individuals with gender dysphoria or non-binary identities often show higher rates of autistic traits compared to the general population (Bruce et al., 2023; Fortunato et al., 2022; Van Der Miesen et al., 2016).

In response to misconceptions that ASC is mainly a male condition, that both males and females with ASC appear to show an exaggeration of the male profile (Baron-Cohen & Hammer, 1997; Baron-Cohen et al., 2005) and that many gender-diverse adults are also autistic, comparison tables were developed in the second study that were designed to illustrate similarities and/or differences of survey responses between the males, females and other groupings who participated in the study. However, since only 0.5% (2 people) selected other, comparisons from this small group were discounted as this low number would not be representative of this population.

Of the 44 participants who took part in the interview stage, ASC participants included 40% (6) females and 60% (9) males whereas NT participants included 93% (27) females and 7% (2) males. The 400 participants in the two studies included 69 males, 329 females and 2 who identified as other. Totals in graphs and tables did not always equal 100% because not every survey statement was answered in each survey and the 'other' category was not included. Not all graphs were developed into comparison tables when the data was not statistically significant.

While a standard gender bias (consistent with research) was found in the survey and interview components in regard to the NT participants, it was not consistent in regard to the interview component with the ASC participants. Smith (2008) found that 'females are more likely to engage in online activity characterised by communication and exchanging of information whereas males are more likely to engage in online activity characterised by seeking of information' (p. 13). Only 14 NT males participated in the survey whereas 238 NT females participated. However, since more autistic males participated in the interview stage of the second study, either more autistic males wanted to talk about their communication difficulties, more females did not want to talk, or more males recognise themselves as autistic compared to females with ASC. While the majority of participants discussed their relationships with their partners, many also discussed their relationships with their adult children, siblings and parents. The participant, who completed two separate surveys (one on her partner, and one on her daughter) discussed both of these relationships.

Evidential Elements

The data analysis processes used in the studies allowed both quantitative (closed-ended), and qualitative (open-ended), data to be brought together, with one data set building on, and extending the other (Sweetman et al., 2010). This procedure allowed for a full exploration of the evidence that could be found on the prompt dependency cycle and the impact it had on communication within these relationships.

The quantitative and qualitative results of both studies, as well as analytic coding processes, were amalgamated in the second study to reveal the development of five themes: affection and connection incompatibilities, prompting triggers, a prompt dependency cycle, additional cycles and three potential outcomes.

Marching to Different Drums

Chapters 2 through to 5 explores the first main theme: 'affection and connection incompatibilities'. This theme explores 'the why' behind the behaviours of prompting, prompt dependency and prompt avoidance in neurodiverse relationships. It highlights situations where people with autism spectrum conditions and neurotypical individuals may have different needs for emotional closeness, which can lead to mismatches. These mismatches, or incompatibilities, often set off a chain of events that can lead to people on the autism spectrum depending on prompts, or avoiding.

Chapters 6 and 7 introduce the concept of 'prompting triggers', while Chapters 8 and 9 examine 'a prompt dependency cycle'. These themes explore 'the what' of prompting and prompt dependency by identifying what conditions cause prompting and prompt dependency (and/or avoidance) to become the main communication strategy within these relationships; what circumstances activate prompting and prompt dependency (and/or avoidance) to form into a dynamic communication cycle; what coping strategies participants use to deal with being entangled in the communication cycle; and what transpires as a result of the choice of coping strategies used.

In particular the second theme, 'prompting triggers', explains how a lack of emotional connection can cause NT participants to initiate prompting. It looks at why prompting becomes their main approach to communication, what purposes it serves, and the outcomes it leads to. The third theme, the 'prompt dependency cycle', describes a communication pattern shaped by a mix of needs and reactions. In this cycle, the desire for connection constantly clashes with the urge to avoid it, creating an ongoing

Have The Numbers Gone Nuts?

tug-of-war. For NT participants, it's about reaching out and wanting interaction, while for ASC participants, it's about either avoiding, or occasionally relying on, prompts to communicate. This dynamic makes conversations unpredictable, as ASC participants might alternate between avoiding and responding to prompts, creating a back-and-forth loop. This cycle is marked by anxiety around conversations for ASC individuals and a need to keep the conversation going for NT participants. Ultimately, this pattern creates a power struggle, with one person trying to maintain things as they are, while the other seeks change. This friction drives the prompt dependency cycle, keeping it in constant motion.

Chapter 10 looks at the fourth theme, 'additional cycles', and Chapter 11 explores the fifth theme, 'three potential relationship outcomes'. These themes examine the impact of the prompt dependency cycle, revealing new cycles of communication that develop because of the ongoing struggle between different needs in these relationships. The back-and-forth of these behaviours alters how conversations happen, leading to unexpected outcomes, and shaping three potential paths for the relationship's future.

In particular the fourth theme, 'additional cycles' shows that the constant recurring behaviours of NT participants prompting and ASC participants either protecting themselves or depending on prompts creates extra communication cycles within the main prompt dependency cycle. This happens because each person has different views on emotional connection, and the resulting cycles develop into the primary way they communicate. Over time, this power struggle to hold on to individual needs and perspectives on connection

Marching to Different Drums

makes these cycles a constant part of their conversations and interactions. The durability of these patterns becomes a defining feature of these relationships, shaping how those within them interact daily.

The fifth theme, 'three potential relationship outcomes', explains what these ongoing communication cycles can mean for couples in neurodiverse relationships. The unfulfilled need for emotional connection, the continuous loop of prompting and response (or lack of response), and the frustration of not fully resolving these differences can create major challenges. This cycle was found to lead to one of three possible outcomes: the relationship may flourish, manage to hold together or start to break down. These paths reflect how deeply the prompt dependency cycle affects the stability and future of the relationship.

These five themes illustrate the unconventionality observed in neurodiverse relationships which is illustrated in the diagram at the bock of the book (see Figure 12.1) The key findings drawn from the survey analysis were based on cross-tabulation and MS Excel analysis of the survey data. To read the complete thesis, type the following link into your browser: http://ro.ecu.edu.au/theses/2292

Chapter Synopsis

This chapter explored the background of two studies that looked into prompt dependency in adults with ASC and how it affects the individuals involved and their relationships. It also discussed how the traits of autism, combined with the usual expectations of neurotypical people and the challenges of close relationships, can lead to prompt dependency. This can create a communication gap that turns into a cycle, making it harder to build fulfilling personal connections. The next chapter looks at 'why' this happens; why prompting, prompt dependency or even prompt avoidance often begins in neurodiverse relationships.

2

An Expressive Divide

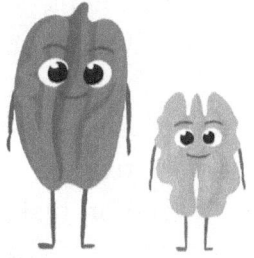

'To effectively communicate, we must realise that we are all different in the way we perceive the world and use this understanding as a guide to our communication with others.'
Anthony Robbins

Have The Numbers Gone Nuts?

It is well established that reciprocity, especially in the social aspects of life, is a major challenge for individuals on the spectrum, and accordingly, reciprocity is difficult to achieve in the circumstance of a neurodiverse relationship. Consistent with research (Kimura et al., 2020), findings from my studies confirmed that for adults involved in a neurodiverse relationship (whether romantic, parent-child or between siblings) the attainment of healthy reciprocal interaction was a highly unlikely occurrence. The core findings of my research were that the low levels of reciprocity in these relationships resulted in a misalliance of needs between the two groups of people. The needs of one, to have reciprocal interaction (NT), conflicted with the needs of the other, to avoid reciprocal interaction (ASC).

As previously stated, it is also well-established that many children on the autism spectrum are dependent on prompts provided by adults for staying on-task, completing activities and transitioning between activities in the home, school and community environments. In addition to uncovering that people on the autism spectrum can continue to require this type of support throughout their lifetime, my research also uncovered various consequences and outcomes that giving and receiving this type of support had on close relationships.

A Remarkable Finding

While prompts are a normal part of life, such as alarms to wake us up in the morning or verbal reminders and notes, in most teaching situations, prompts are used as a temporary learning aid when precise step-by-step instruction is required. Prompting is designed to help children respond correctly during the acquisition phase of learning when they need extra help. However, prompt dependence means that a person becomes dependent on the prompt to perform a particular behaviour. The behaviour and prompt become linked and independent behaviour does not develop. A lack of independent behaviour can contribute to learned helplessness and the belief that one's own behaviour does not control outcomes or results (Sternberg & Williams, 2010). In that case, ongoing prompting may then be required every time that behaviour is required.

Findings from my studies established that the incompatibility between the needs of each in neurodiverse relationships was the main cause for the onset of prompting on the part of NT participants, and prompt avoidance and/or prompt dependency on the part of ASC participants. In the context of close relationships, it was confirmed that adults on the spectrum require prompts provided by their significant others to guide and direct them throughout life, especially in the social and emotional aspects.

During the course of the two studies, it was discovered that there is a pattern to how prompting (NT) and a dependency on or avoidance of the prompts (ASC) develop in the context of neurodiverse relationships. By looking closely at specific moments in the data, it was found that differences in communication abilities and differences in emotional needs cause participants with ASC to attempt to avoid emotional communication. Their need for these aspects also tends to be lower than typical populations. At the same time, NT participants showed a higher interactive capability and a higher need for emotional communication in their relationships than those on the spectrum. This contrast means that in the context of a neurodiverse relationship, the higher need for emotional communication can remain unmet. Prompting by NT participants was found to be the main way to attempt to overturn this unmet need. However, a low need for emotional communication led those with ASC to, either rely heavily on the prompts, or actively avoid them. This needs disparity is the rationale behind the development of prompting (NT) and a dependency on or avoidance of the prompts (ASC) to become linked in the context of neurodiverse relationships.

These incompatibilities between the two groups of participants were found to be constant. By examining specific instances within the data that shed light on these incompatibilities, it was found that the linked behaviours of prompting and dependency on (or avoidance of) the prompts trigger a chain of events that not only cause these behaviours to cycle between the people in these relationships, but also to cause additional communicational cycles to form between them. By combining answers to survey questions with written responses from surveys and interviews from both studies, I was able to gather prevalence data, make the findings more applicable to a broader audience, and uncover the story behind why this pattern occurred.

The Formula

It is well-established in research that autistic people experience difficulties expressing emotions and conversing about personal and emotional matters. The survey and interview data in my studies confirmed these research findings (Attwood, 2015; Lorant, 2011; Moreno et al., 2012). It emerged that the main contributing factor to a lack of affectionate, deep and meaningful conversations within neurodiverse relationships, was that participants with ASC often avoided expressing feelings and emotions, conversing about personal matters and habitually resisted deep and meaningful conversations. Responses to survey items (SI) show the different reasonings of each group of participants.

The Emotional Divide

When looking at the answers to SI 13 and SI 15 (Figures 2.1 and 2.2), there's a noticeable difference in how ASC and NT respondents feel about expressing emotions. Out of 107 people with ASC who responded to SI 13, 66% said it wasn't easy for them to communicate their feelings (Figure 2.1). On the other hand, NT respondents had a much easier time. Out of 252 responses, 86% said they always or mostly found it easy to express their emotions (Figure 2.1).

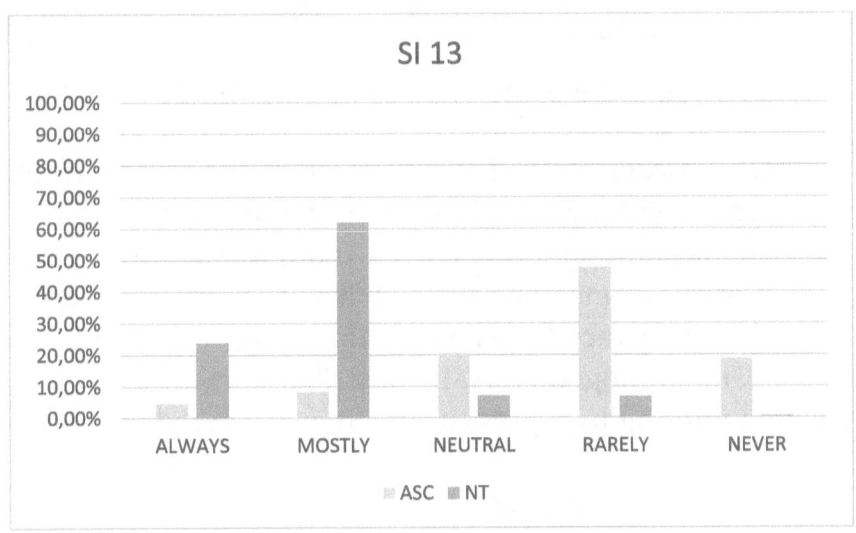

Figure 2.1. SI 13. I find it easy to communicate what I am feeling.

Have The Numbers Gone Nuts?

Both males and females with ASC expressed a similar difficulty with expressing emotions. Table 2.1 shows that the majority of both males and females with ASC said they rarely or never found it easy to communicate their emotions whereas less than 15% of both male and female NT respondents said they had trouble expressing their feelings. It is interesting to note that in the NT population, the ease of communication about feelings transcends any male-female differences.

	ASC Female	%	ASC Male	%	NT Female	%	NT Male	%
Always	4	6	1	2.5	59	25	1	7
Mostly	4	6	5	12.5	146	61	10	71
Neutral	16	25	6	15	17	7	1	7
Rarely	29	45	21	52.5	15	6	2	14
Never	12	18	7	17.5	1	.4	0	0
Total	65		40		238		14	

Table 2.1. I find it easy to communicate what I am feeling.

Interviewees shared more about these differences. Participants with ASC said they found it difficult to express their feelings and emotions. Even though they knew their partner or family members wanted them to open up more, the difficulties they faced often made them want to avoid these conversations altogether. Wally described this difficulty and what attempting to express his feelings triggered for him:

I express it by saying I don't want to talk about this because I'll get upset ... Trying to identify what the feeling is and how to deal with it is really hard and it gets in the way of rationality.

An Expressive Divide

Similarly, Rachelle explained how limiting emotional conversations functioned well for her, while acknowledging that her partner was not satisfied:

> *Well, it meets my needs, I'm happy just to have ... even just a 10-minute conversation a day and that forms for me a good marriage, but he wants more constant connection throughout the day. He doesn't feel satisfied.*

William inadvertently conveyed the message that he chose not to put effort into understanding and decoding the expectations and needs of others:

> *But as an NT, you seem to appreciate the social interaction where I couldn't care less. I just do it because you're expected to, you have to. It's just an interruption and an annoyance.*

Mary questioned why it was even necessary to interact and communicate affection, stating that she preferred inanimate objects for that reason:

> *Like I don't understand why people tell each other that they love each other all the time. You say it once and that's what you mean. If the parameters don't change then why do you need to say it again, because you have already told them ... I love my carefully contact-wrapped, beautifully preserved ... book collection as much as I love people. It is the same kind of love ... and it is sometimes easier to love the inanimate because I don't have to interact.*

Malcolm described the challenges of conveying feelings:

Have The Numbers Gone Nuts?

She will say 'Oh honey, tell me how you are feeling.' And of course, to me as an Aspie, I have got nothing to talk to you about. Just like saying, 'Can you speak some Russian to me?' And I will say 'Honey, I can't answer that. I have got nothing to say to you.' Like I will talk spontaneously, if planet Malcolm is in the right position, but that is it, and of course, she finds that challenging.

Samuel explained why he didn't want to be involved in emotional discussions:

It would be far too intense for me to cope with ... so mostly, no I don't really want emotional discussions because things usually end up causing a fight and usually end up escalating.

Likewise, Tom revealed anxiety led him to avoid emotional conversations:

I prefer to keep to myself or talk about topics that are interesting to me. Emotive conversations make me feel anxious.

NT participants acknowledged that they understood the difficulties their partner or family members faced. However, this understanding didn't take away their disappointment. They felt that the lack of these conversations led to fewer meaningful interactions and a weaker sense of connection. Winnie described how conversations became 'stilted' when focused on emotions:

Sharing of emotions is not something that we do very often or with a great deal of depth ... if I ask him how he is feeling he won't respond to those sorts of questions... he cannot

An Expressive Divide

express how he is feeling and similarly if I express how I am feeling his understanding is very limited ... so that makes our conversations quite stilted around emotions.

Similarly, Maggie reported her son's difficulty with expressing emotions:

I know he feels love ... but he doesn't know how to integrate the expected expressions of love into a normal kind of interaction.

Although Nora's understanding was evident, so was her dissatisfaction:

Obviously, I'd prefer to have more ... of my intimate relational needs satisfied by him ... but his capacity is not at my capacity of ... relating ... so that's where my dissatisfaction ... comes [from].

Ruth shared exchanges of information replaced emotional conversation:

I would not describe my husband as warm or affectionate ... Displays of affection or any declarations of love or affection are foreign and make him feel uncomfortable ... Most of our conversations are exchanges of information.

Most participants with ASC answered that they preferred to stick to less emotional conversations, while NT participants preferred the opposite. Out of 107 ASC survey responses to the statement 'I would prefer to keep to less emotive conversations', 66% agreed, 24% were neutral and only 9% disagreed (Figure 2.2). On the other hand, NT participants were more likely to prefer emotional conversations. Of the 252 NT respondents, 68% said they rarely or never preferred less emotional conversations, 25% were neutral and only 7% said they mostly preferred less emotional discussions (Figure 2.2).

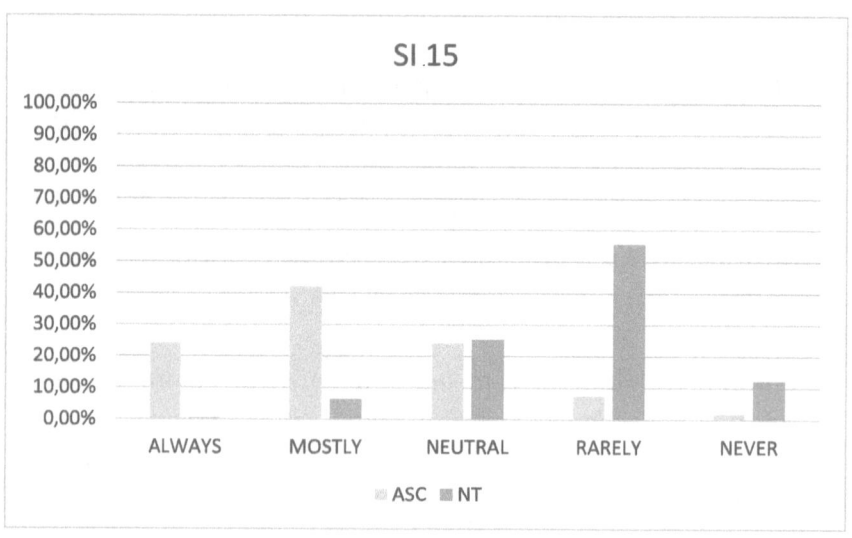

Figure 2.2. SI 15. I would prefer to keep to less emotive conversations.

Most males and females with ASC showed a similar preference for less emotional conversations, while most NT males and females showed a similar preference for more emotional conversations (Table 2.2).

An Expressive Divide

	ASC Female	%	ASC Male	%	NT Female	%	NT Male	%
Always	16	25	10	25	1	.42	0	0
Mostly	27	42	17	42.5	13	5	3	21
Neutral	16	25	9	22.5	60	25	4	29
Rarely	5	8	3	7.5	133	56	7	50
Never	1	2	1	2.5	31	13	0	0
Total	65		40		238		14	

Table 2.2. I would prefer to keep to less emotive conversations.

Comments from the survey also confirmed similar positions toward emotive conversations between the males and females within each group of participants. A female respondent with ASC said:

I have great difficulty communicating my emotional state.

A male respondent with ASC said:

I find it hard to process/think about, relationship/feelings stuff.

In contrast, an NT female respondent said:

[I] have to be more rational and not emotive at all. As soon as any emotion is involved, he shuts down.

An NT male respondent said:

It's become second nature, now, to avoid emotional responses and getting angry ... everything will escalate, and the situation will be dreadful for many days. It's better to remain factual and emotionally neutral.

Both male and female ASC participants showed a preference for an impassive type of interaction:

> SAMUEL *We would tend to get overly emotional and not know when to stop and things would rapidly spiral out of hand into a fight ... and Sally would insist on continuing the conversation until it drove me nuts.*

> RACHELLE *I'm quite happy to sit in silence ... [Emotional conversation is] too confusing and I don't understand it.*

Some NT respondents chose 'neutral' or said they mostly preferred less emotional conversations. In their interviews, they explained that this was specifically about emotional conversations with their ASC partner or family member. They had either stopped trying to have these types of conversations or significantly reduced them. During the interviews, it became clear that many NT participants felt frustrated by the lack of emotional expression from their ASC partner or family member. They found it hard to handle and needed more emotional engagement to feel secure in the relationship. Without it, they often felt insecure and rejected. Over time, many realised that trying to connect emotionally led to disappointment, so they often chose to avoid emotional conversations altogether. Wanda expressed the widely held position within the NT group:

An Expressive Divide

I try to not express too much emotion in what I might say. So, in conversations if I think that I'm not being understood, these days, I tend to just back out of the conversation.

The majority of NT participants also lamented the absence of closeness with their significant other, and what the resulting lack of affection meant to them:

TRACY — *When I get close to him to express my emotions and my love, he is not ready to receive or to accept me, as if he is rejecting me. I asked him not to remain like an ice cube, without acknowledging my presence, when I approach him.*

NORA — *I can't need stuff emotionally from him and if I do it has to be like I can't be emotional about it ... but I think the bottom line is just move on, just get over it.*

RONDA — *The closer I would try to get the more he would run away ... unconsciously to me ... [it seems] talking with me is not desirable; being around me is not desirable.*

DIANNE — *He doesn't show anything, like there is no emotion. Like not even a touch or a hug, or a 'It will be okay', or a recognition even that you are hurting, even though it's got to be obvious that you are.*

Have The Numbers Gone Nuts?

The Personal Divide

The survey and interview data showed that communication challenges faced by autistic people impacted their desire to express feelings and emotions. ASC participants shared in their interviews that they preferred to keep conversations more factual and less personal because expressing emotions made them feel uncertain and anxious. On the other hand, NT participants rarely had trouble with emotional conversations. They enjoyed more expressive, emotional and personal interactions and were naturally inclined to make conversations more intimate.

The ability to convey the meaning behind emotional exchanges is key when talking about personal matters. It was found that the differences between ASC and NT participants in understanding what their conversational partners meant also affected a willingness to discuss personal topics. Frequently, ASC participants were found to misinterpret the meaning behind what was being said, and as interactions became entangled it caused a two-way miscommunication. The resulting entangled exchanges led to disagreements and created tension. To avoid these misunderstandings and the conflicts that followed, ASC participants tended to try and evade personal conversations altogether.

The survey results confirmed these differences, showing that autistic respondents struggled more with communicating meaning than their NT counterparts. Of the 107 autistic respondents, 75% acknowledged having difficulties with conveying meaning (Figure 2.3). In contrast, among the 252 NT respondents, 73% said that issues with communicating meaning were rare or did not happen (Figure 2.3).

An Expressive Divide

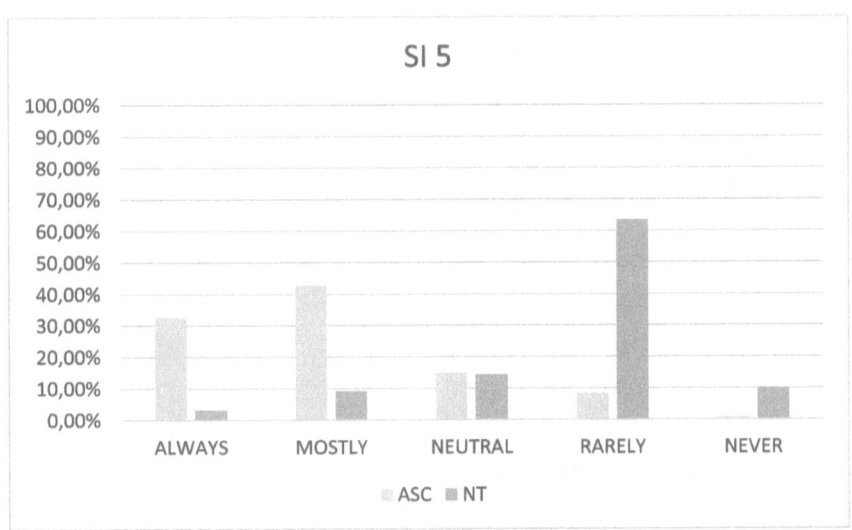

Figure 2.3. SI 5. Communicating the real meaning of what I am talking about is difficult.

Both male and female autistic respondents showed similar difficulties in this area (Table 2.3). For example, a female survey respondent with ASC commented that:

Misunderstandings ... escalate due to very different communication/thinking styles ... I have [a] precise, analytical and often pedantic thinking style.

However, both male and female NT respondents showed that, for the most part, they did not have these difficulties.

Have The Numbers Gone Nuts?

	ASC Female	%	ASC Male	%	NT Female	%	NT Male	%
Always	20	31	13	32.5	7	3	1	7
Mostly	26	40	20	50	22	9	1	7
Neutral	14	22	2	5	32	13	4	29
Rarely	5	8	4	10	152	64	8	57
Never	0	0	1	2.5	25	10.5	0	0
Total	65		40		238		14	

Table 2.3. Communicating the real meaning of what I am talking about is difficult.

Most ASC participants felt that having personal conversations, which are often expected in close relationships, was an unwelcome challenge, made harder by difficulties in communicating meaning. Edith explained the different ways she attempted to make sense of what she wanted to say, as opposed to her NT partner:

> *I actually have to talk it through and then I understand what it is ... and so for him it is inefficient, for me it's the process ... because I haven't fully formed what I'm thinking about ... then he's in the situation of not understanding what I'm thinking, not necessarily liking the process that he's forced to go through to find out what I'm thinking ... the thinking and the feeling are separate.*

Since conversations with their autistic partners and family members often felt difficult and confusing, most NT participants also found personal conversations to be an unwelcome task. The struggles their partners and family members had with expressing feelings and emotions often led to misunderstandings, leaving both sides unclear about what was really being said. Sally explained the tangled communication that ensued when attempting to clarify her meaning to her partner with ASC:

I can't tell him what I'm trying to tell him, because he won't listen and ... it's really hard to get him to focus on what I'm actually trying to say, and what's important to me ... what I am actually trying to get across, and trying to explain tends to get completely lost in all the words missing, and the exaggerating, and the going off on tangents, and he interrupts me all the time ... so I don't feel heard.

The Meaningful Divide

The differences in the need for emotional connection in neurodiverse relationships led to a clear lack of deep, meaningful conversations. As shown in Figures 2.4 and 2.5, the survey data revealed that both ASC and NT respondents agreed that deep conversations are important for building closeness in relationships (Figure 2.4). However, many felt that these conversations were missing in their own relationships (Figure 2.5).

A total of 65% autistic respondents and 92% NT respondents said that having deep, meaningful conversations was always or mostly important for close relationships (Figure 2.4). However, 49% autistic respondents and 70% NT respondents admitted that they rarely had these kinds of conversations in their relationships (Figure 2.5).

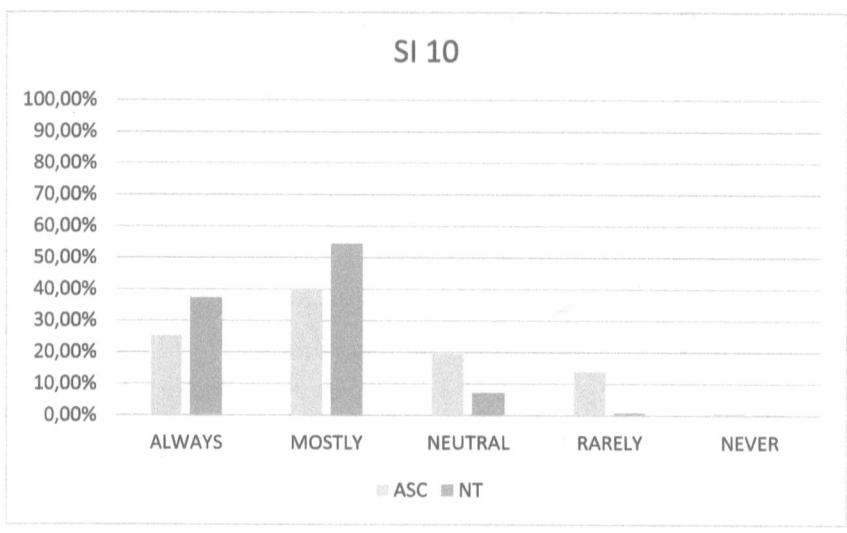

Figure 2.4. SI 10. The best way for me to experience close connections with others is to have deep, meaningful conversations with them.

The results shown in table 2.4 reveals very little difference between males and females within each group. While both ASC and NT participants recognised the importance of deep conversations, a higher percentage of NT participants than ASC participants selected always or mostly. It is interesting to note that a third of male ASC respondents selected neutral (Table 2.4).

An Expressive Divide

	ASC Female	%	ASC Male	%	NT Female	%	NT Male	%
Always	19	29	7	17.5	88	37	6	43
Mostly	30	46	12	30	130	55	7	50
Neutral	8	12	13	32.5	18	8	0	0
Rarely	8	12	7	17.5	1	.5	1	.5
Never	0	0	1	2.5	1	.5	0	0
Total	65		40		238		14	

Table 2.4. The best way for me to experience close connections with others is to have deep, meaningful conversations with them.

The statement in Figure 2.5 evaluates the one in Figure 2.4. These graphs show that while ASC participants understand the importance of meaningful conversations for building close relationships (Figure 2.4), this awareness doesn't always translate into actually having those conversations (Figure 2.5). The data in Figure 2.4 aligns more with what NT interviewees reported, rather than what autistic interviewees shared. This means that while autistic participants intellectually understand the need for deep, meaningful conversations, their interviews revealed that this understanding did not always lead to taking action.

Have The Numbers Gone Nuts?

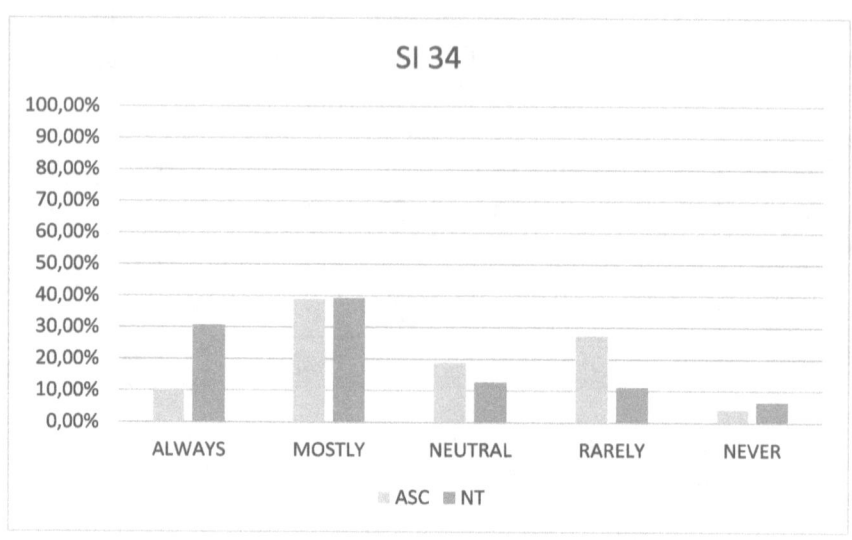

Figure 2.5. SI 34. Deep and meaningful conversations do not take place.

The results shown in table 2.5 shows that most ASC and NT males and females agreed with each other that deep and meaningful conversations do not take place in their relationships.

An Expressive Divide

	ASC Female	%	ASC Male	%	NT Female	%	NT Male	%
Always	6	11	4	11	74	32	1	7
Mostly	19	35	16	42	89	39	7	50
Neutral	13	24	5	13	29	13	2	14
Rarely	14	25	12	32	24	10	3	21
Never	3	5	3	3	15	6	1	7
Total	55		38		231		14	

Table 2.5. Deep and meaningful conversations do not take place.

A survey respondent with ASC confirmed that while he understood the necessity of having deeper conversations, he struggled to accomplish it:

Communicating about internal feelings is difficult for me, and I often have difficulty responding to questions in deeper conversations. Don't understand myself and my desires in order to share them. I don't think I 'get' relationships and personal intimacy – may know the theory but struggle to apply it. I have great difficulty meeting my wife's needs and find it difficult to change my patterns of behaviour and conversation.

An NT survey respondent shared the NT perspective on the difficulty that the ASC survey respondent noted:

I have explained to my partner that the way I feel connected to him is through talking and that it is hard for me to maintain a feeling of connectedness when he barely responds. He made more effort for a while but seems to have given up. Perhaps it is too hard. I try cognitively

Have The Numbers Gone Nuts?

to value all the actions he does which show me he cares, because he does do lots of nice things for me, but somehow, they don't mean as much to me as a conversation. I have to deliberately think about the things he does and place value on them. There is not the automatic satisfaction that comes with a meaningful conversation.

Not only did ASC participants report a preference for more of an objective, logical type of interaction, but some conveyed dissatisfaction with the necessity of also having to participate within meaningful conversations. Wally shared that he understood the importance of meaningful conversations, and revealed the reasons that he avoided them:

I have an intellectual belief that it's important to be able to have that deep exchange of ideas and … a respect that other people's feelings are different, and I understand that that's a necessity so … of course it would be better to do this, but it's a scary place to go … so I will avoid.

Similarly, while recognising its importance, Tom disclosed his dislike of meaningful conversation:

I recognise the necessity of having meaningful conversations if I want a close connection. However, I do not like this type of conversation.

On the other hand, Sharon identified the features that conveyed meaningful conversation for her:

Warm and affectionate conversations in my context translate into deep and meaningful intellectual discourse that may or may not involve our feelings for each other.

An Expressive Divide

Generally, NT participants lamented the lack of deep, meaningful conversation that they required for emotional connectedness. Tracy shared what she had put in the survey and why:

I answered in the questionnaire that I was never satisfied with our emotional connection now, simply because there is none.

Likewise, Sabrina shared a similar sentiment, labelling her relationship as a business relationship:

There's just no more affection left. It's truly a business relationship ... It's just day-to-day things that anybody would deal with but there's no emotion, there's just none.

Beth described the complexity in attempting to hold important conversations:

He can get onto the one topic and just go on and on and on and I'll have to change the subject. I'll have to say, 'Now look I've got to discuss this with you, it's really important.'

Tracy described the impacts on her of an absence of deep, meaningful conversation within her relationship:

[My partner] does not understand what I am after. He doesn't know why I would not feel 'close' to him ... I have just stopped trying to have deep and meaningful conversations with him ... I end up having those conversations with other people, friends or my children.

A Collision of More with Less

The survey and interview data confirmed earlier research (Attwood, 2015; Ekman & Hiltunen, 2015) showing that people with ASC often rely on avoidance behaviours. Although these behaviours stem from communication difficulties, autistic participants frequently avoided expressing emotions, talking about personal matters and engaging in deep, meaningful conversations. This avoidance often led to lower levels of affection in their relationships, which in turn caused disagreements between autistic and NT individuals over expectations and viewpoints about amounts of affection given and received.

A total of 42% ASC respondents admitted that warm, affectionate conversations were lacking in their relationships (Figure 2.6), but 46% said they were satisfied with the current level of affection and rarely or never wanted more (Figure 2.7). In contrast, 84% of NT respondents agreed that their relationships lacked warm, affectionate conversations (Figure 2.6), and 75% often or always wanted more affection (Figure 2.7).

An Expressive Divide

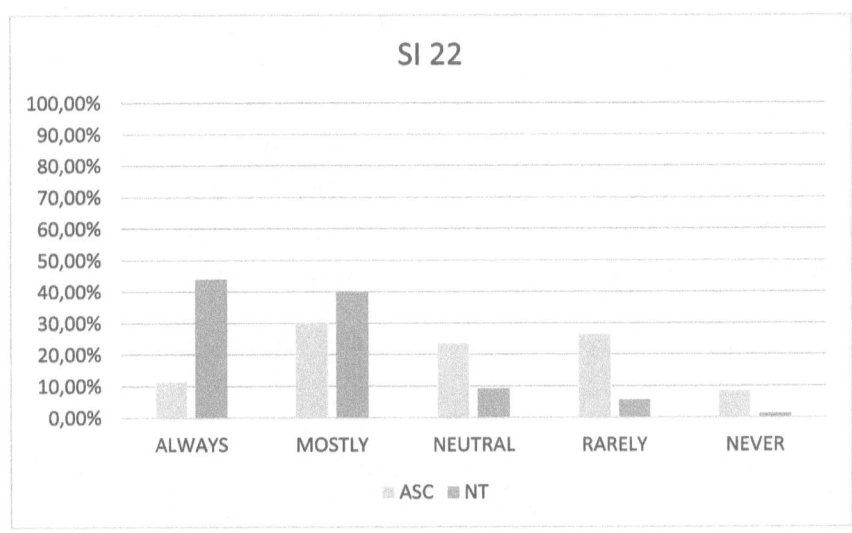

Figure 2.6. SI 22. I feel that warm, affectionate conversations are lacking.

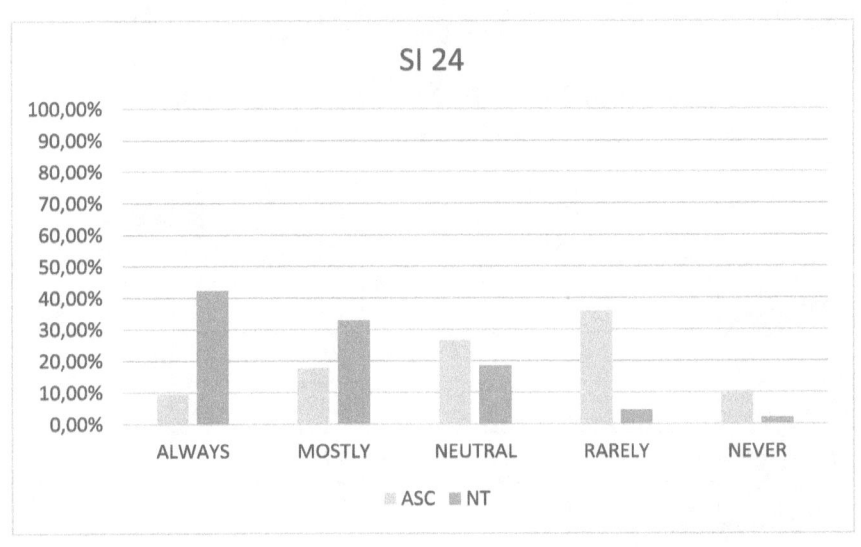

Figure 2.7. SI 24. I want more affection expressed.

Have The Numbers Gone Nuts?

While a larger percentage of autistic females than males felt that affectionate conversations were lacking (Table 2.6), both autistic females and males showed a similar preference for lower levels of expressed affection (Table 2.7). In agreement with autistic participants, both NT males and females felt that affectionate conversations were lacking (Table 2.6), however both the NT females and males wanted more expressed affection (Table 2.7).

	ASC Female	%	ASC Male	%	NT Female	%	NT Male	%
Always	8	12	4	10	107	45	3	21
Mostly	17	26	15	38	93	37	7	50
Neutral	15	23	9	23	20	10	3	21
Rarely	20	31	8	21	13	5	1	7
Never	5	8	3	8	3	3	0	0
Total	65		39		236		14	

Table 2.6. I feel that warm, affectionate conversations are lacking.

	ASC Female	%	ASC Male	%	NT Female	%	NT Male	%
Always	8	12	2	5	103	44	3	21
Mostly	10	15	9	23	74	31	8	57
Neutral	14	22	13	33	43	18	3	21
Rarely	27	42	11	28	11	5	0	0
Never	6	9	4	10	5	2	0	0
Total	65		39		236		14	

Table 2.7. I want more affection expressed.

An Expressive Divide

The interview data confirmed what the survey data showed, that NT participants had a greater need for affectionate conversations in their close relationships compared to those with ASC. Most interviewees with ASC said that while they noticed their partner/family members' need for affection, they didn't feel the same need themselves:

WALLY   *Well we don't have the kind of rituals that I observe in others ... We've been married nearly 30 years and we've never had the things that other people express ... for example, in the habit of a kiss goodbye on the way out in the morning, even the 'Honey I'm home' is a stereotype which doesn't apply. It's just never been something that we do.*

SANDRA   *I do know that he wishes that we would be more affectionate with each other and ... I guess I don't have that feeling as much.*

MURRAY   *Yeah, I think it's more, I understand intellectually it's the right thing to do. I think 'Oh it's been a couple of months since I bought flowers, I should buy flowers.'*

TERRY   *Quite often she'll just come up and hug me, sometimes without notice, so I'm learning to accept that and for me a good hug is probably anything up to a minute probably, but 2 or 3 minutes is something I'm learning to adapt to, or longer.*

Have The Numbers Gone Nuts?

On the other hand, although the majority of NT participants said that they noticed their partner/family members with ASC did not seem to have the same needs, they lamented the lack of affectionate and deep, meaningful conversation within their relationships. They spoke about the resulting lack of emotional connection and what it meant for them in their relationship:

QUINN   *It's kind of hard for my husband to connect with me emotionally ... it doesn't matter if I tell him this is what I need, however many times, he doesn't seem to be able to get to the level that I need him to be.*

TRACY   *But with time, I stopped trying to have deep conversations with [my partner] because I went away empty each time ... In the end, you try to protect yourself from constant disappointment.*

MAGGIE   *Whenever I want to talk about anything that's emotional, [my husband] will either shut down or just change the subject ... I'm closer to some of my friends, I have better communication with my friends ... but I have my daughter, I have my husband, there's a chance that my son-in-law has, and there's a chance that my grandson has, so [I'm] surround[ed by] AS. I can't hold and give to every single one of them.*

RUTH   *I know he loves me, but he does not feel love in the same way I do. He has reported that love*

An Expressive Divide

as an emotion is a big gaping hole to him. He doesn't really know what it feels like, but he 'loves' me in his own way.

Chapter Synopsis

This chapter started the discussion about the first theme: affection and connection incompatibilities. It looked into why prompting and prompt dependency often emerges in neurodiverse relationships. The findings explained that since people with ASC and neurotypical individuals tend to approach emotions, personal topics and deep conversations in very different ways, these differences can lead to a noticeable disconnect between the two groups.

The next chapter takes this theme a step further by exploring how fear plays into these dynamics. It explains how fear can heighten the mismatched needs for affection and connection, making the gaps between ASC and NT individuals in neurodiverse relationships even more significant.

3

A Stranglehold

'Thinking will not overcome fear but action will.'
W Clement Stone

Have The Numbers Gone Nuts?

Considerable research has established that people on the autism spectrum often experience high levels of anxiety due to the complications they have with social interaction (Ainsworth et al., 2020; Dubin, 2009; Lamport & Zlomke, 2014). Studies show that up to 50% of autistic individuals experience social anxiety, much higher than the 7–13% seen in the general population. Along with this, autistic individuals face many unique and ongoing challenges in their daily lives. Their difficulties with communication, such as understanding social cues, making eye contact, interpreting body language or holding conversations, can lead to high levels of anxiety in social situations. This social anxiety is different from the typical social awkwardness others may feel as it can often be more intense and harder to manage.

Since autistic people tend to prefer predictable environments and can struggle with uncertainty or change (Jenkinson et al., 2020), the unpredictability of social situations can often worsen their anxieties. The combination of severe anxiety and prevalent difficulties can lead to intense fears, especially when based on past negative experiences. Memories of setbacks and past problems can shape how mistakes are viewed, fuelling a growing fear of failure and causing cycles of self-doubt and anxiety. This fear of failure can make people on the spectrum hesitant to try new things or step outside of their comfort zone, either becoming inflexible or sometimes leading to what is known as learned helplessness.

Learned helplessness occurs when someone feels unable to solve problems that are actually within their ability to solve, due to their patterns of thinking and behaviour (Lowenstein, 2012). In other words, learned helplessness is a mindset that can be internalised when anxiety-provoking situations are repeatedly encountered which are unable to be prevented. This mindset can result in giving up, becoming passive and shutting down.

The survey and interview data corroborated these research findings. The challenges of navigating emotional conversations, and the frustrations of resulting miscommunications led many participants with ASC to avoid interactions. Many also discussed how a fear of failure led them to choose various avoidance behaviours.

Anxiety's Assault

The survey confirmed that people with ASC often deal with high levels of anxiety, especially when it comes to talking with others. Interviews helped explain the different reasons behind this anxiety and how people manage it. The survey also showed that while most people with autism felt anxious during conversations, this was rarely the case for NT individuals (Figures 3.1 and 3.2). A total of 68% of the ASC respondents said they always or mostly feel anxious when talking to others (Figure 3.1). In contrast, only 7% of NT respondents felt the same, with 82% reporting little or no anxiety during conversations. When it came to personal conversations, 65% of ASC participants said they always or mostly feel anxious, while 56% of NT respondents said they rarely or never feel anxious (Figure 3.2).

Have The Numbers Gone Nuts?

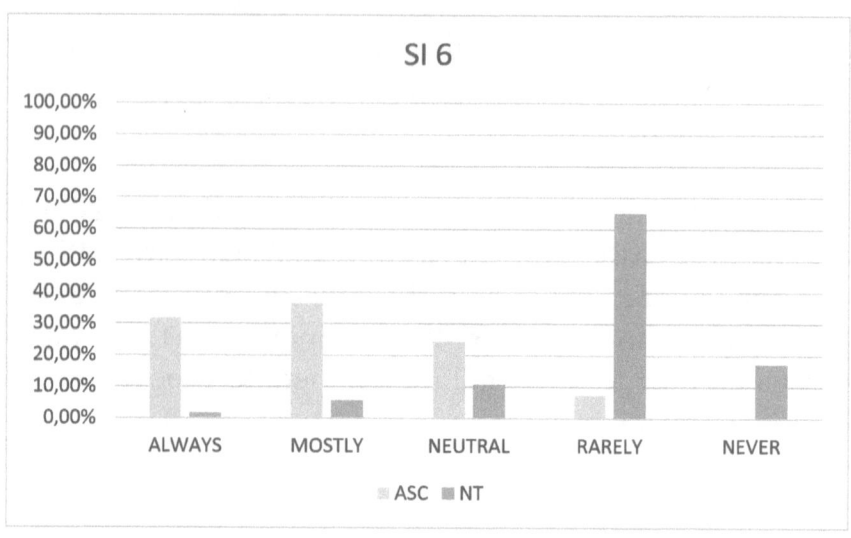

Figure 3.1. SI 6. Talking with others increases my anxiety levels.

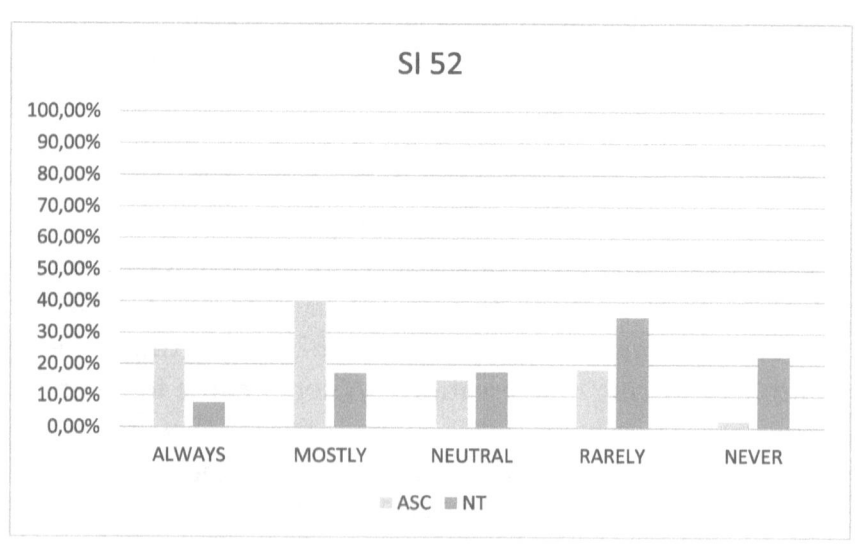

Figure 3.2. SI 52. I feel anxious as soon as conversations become personal.

A Stranglehold

There was no significant difference in responses between men and women in either group but there was a noticeable difference in the experience of anxiety between the ASC and NT groups (Tables 3.1 and 3.2). Autistic females and males showed that they experienced high levels of anxiety in conversations whereas the results in these tables show that the experience of anxiety in these types of conversations was rarely an issue for the NT population.

	ASC Female	%	ASC Male	%	NT Female	%	NT Male	%
Always	25	38	8	20	3	1	1	7
Mostly	23	35	15	37	13	5	1	7
Neutral	14	22	12	30	26	11	1	7
Rarely	3	5	5	12	154	65	10	71
Never	0	0	0	0	42	18	1	7
Total	65		40		238		14	

Table 3.1. Talking with others increases my anxiety levels.

	ASC Female	%	ASC Male	%	NT Female	%	NT Male	%
Always	13	25	10	26	16	7	3	21
Mostly	20	38	16	42	38	16	4	29
Neutral	9	17	5	13	41	188	2	14
Rarely	10	19	6	16	81	35	5	36
Never	1	2	1	3	55	24	0	0
Total	53		38		231		14	

Table 3.2. I feel anxious as soon as conversations become personal.

Have The Numbers Gone Nuts?

Anxiety's Hold

Research shows that anxiety disorders are the most common mental health issue for autistic adults. In fact, the anxiety they experience can sometimes feel more overwhelming than the core traits of autism itself (Ainsworth et al., 2020). As discussed in Books 1 and 2, many participants with autism reported frequent feelings of anxiety, stemming from a fear of failure, the challenges of navigating emotional conversations and the frustrations of miscommunications. These factors were found to be the primary sources of stress, anxiety and a sense of helplessness for them. Sandra (ASC) explained why some conversations caused her to feel anxious:

If it's not emotional, it's ... easier to have a conversation about it. Emotional ones I start to kind of think what I should be doing or what the other person wants me to be saying and trying to really understand and listen to the other person, because I know it's an important thing at that moment ... I have to be more mindful of the connection between us at the moment and what I'm doing and if that seems okay in the situation and there's more thought about my actions and my words ... because I think I'm more kind of anxious about me saying the right thing.

Beth (NT) explained that sometimes she needs to take the blame to manage Christopher's (ASC) anxiety:

If it's become unproductive, I'll just say look I think we're going to have to talk about this again later, we're not going anywhere at the moment. If he's too far gone in his anxiety, then we'll have to keep nutting it out and sometimes I'll just go 'Okay. You're right. I'm wrong. I'm the idiot here. We'll just leave it', but that's when his anxiety is really ramped up, yeah.

Renee (NT) noted that Patrick (ASC) relied on scripts to deal with his stress:

When he's particularly stressed, he'll go back to the script which is this one that he's got and no matter how you try and kind of change that or talk to him about it or whatever, it just keeps coming back. It's the same old stuff.

When asked how she dealt with it, she answered:

What I do, again it depends on the level of his anxiety and if I notice, you've just got to take all the emotion out of it, you can't be upset ... I can't talk to him if I was upset about something because he just doesn't cope with that, so I have learned that I take the emotion out of it, be very clear about what I want to say and if he's really stressed, I won't talk about it until a day or two later which again I know is not ideal but that's how it is really.

Chapter Synopsis

This chapter continued exploring the first theme by showing how a fear of failure, struggles with emotional conversations and frustrations from miscommunications all contribute to the different feelings about giving and receiving affectionate conversations for those on the spectrum. It also highlighted how these issues increase the disconnect in

Have The Numbers Gone Nuts?

neurodiverse relationships. The next chapter continues investigating this theme by taking a closer look at how these growing differences affect the dynamics between the two groups in neurodiverse relationships.

4

A Needs Divide

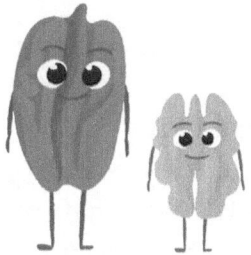

'If there was any great lesson in life it was this: no battle was ever won with silence.'
Shannon L Alder

Have The Numbers Gone Nuts?

People naturally desire connection and the feeling of being cared for. It is an essential element of being human. Baumeister and Leary (1995) called this desire as the 'need to belong'. However, forming strong, healthy relationships is not something we are born knowing how to do. Building this kind of connection takes time, practice and a genuine effort to interact with others. Through these interactions, we learn the skills to connect deeply and handle the many differences that come with each person's unique personality, beliefs and life experiences. Ultimately, it is these shared efforts that make meaningful relationships possible.

On the other hand, since anxiety was reported to be a common theme for autistic participants due to difficulties in identifying and understanding emotions as well as difficulties with giving and receiving emotional communication, these difficulties and the fear that interconnects with these difficulties were found to impact on the ability to form a healthy relationship. Withdrawing from engaging socially was a common theme for those on the spectrum. Given that their difficulties were found to lead to a frequent need to avoid most forms of emotional communication with their partners and family members, it was found that the resulting lack of affectionate and deep, meaningful conversations was the cause of much discord in neurodiverse relationships.

Together Apart

The challenges that autistic people have with expressing emotions, discussing personal or emotional topics, and getting their point across were key reasons why autistic participants often felt the need to escape from conversations

A Needs Divide

with partners or family members. The data revealed that ASC participants mainly used three main strategies to disengage from personal conversations. These were: endeavouring to keep things simple and surface level when spending time with others, seeking alone time to recharge or focusing on their special interests.

The Need for Surface-Level Company

The ASC participants showed that while they do need companionship, they want to experience it differently to NT participants. They enjoy being around others but prefer not to engage in deep or emotionally expressive conversations. Figure 4.1 highlights how the two groups express affection differently. According to the data, 74% of autistic participants felt that affection is best shown through actions rather than words and 46% said they often communicate through their actions (Figures 4.1 and 4.2). In comparison, NT participants were more divided. While 36% agreed that actions are better than words, 37% were neutral and 26% disagreed. Responses to SI 48 reveal that NT participants were more inclined toward verbal communication, with 52% disagreeing that actions are better, 36% staying neutral and 12% agreeing (Figure 4.2).

Have The Numbers Gone Nuts?

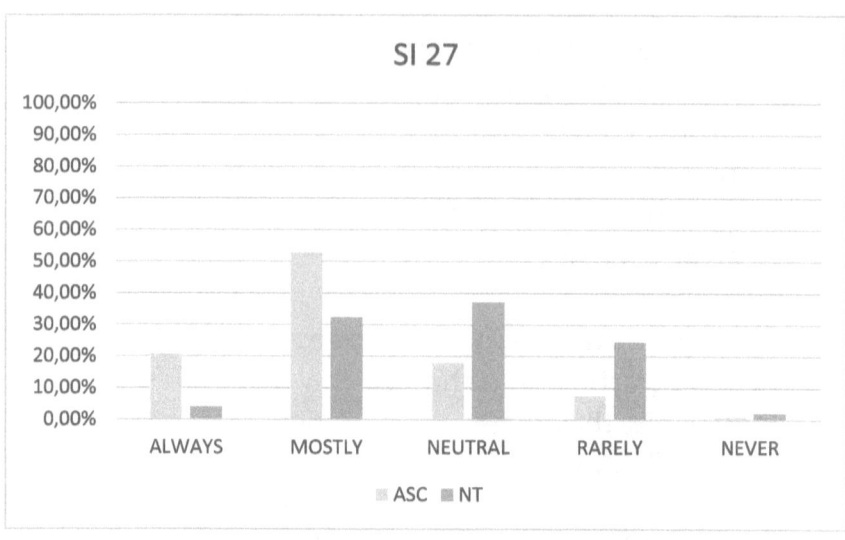

Figure 4.1. SI 27. I think the best way to demonstrate affection is through deeds (that is, actions rather than words).

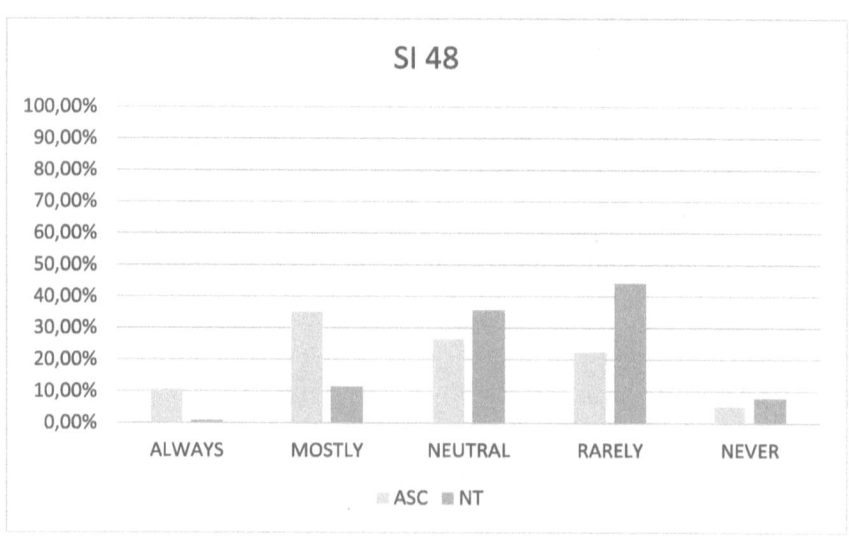

Figure 4.2. SI 48. I communicate by actions rather than by talking.

A Needs Divide

Both male and female respondents with ASC revealed a clear preference for showing affection through actions rather than words (Tables 4.1 and 4.2). In contrast, while NT males and females showed some differences in how they preferred to express affection (Table 4.1), they generally leaned towards using words rather than actions (Table 4.2).

	ASC Female	%	ASC Male	%	NT Female	%	NT Male	%
Always	14	22	7	18	10	4	0	0
Mostly	31	48	24	62	74	31	7	50
Neutral	11	17	8	21	90	38	3	21
Rarely	8	12	0	0	57	24	4	29
Never	1	2	0	0	5	2	0	0
Total	65		39		236		14	

Table 4.1. I think the best way to demonstrate affection is through deeds (that is, actions rather than words).

	ASC Female	%	ASC Male	%	NT Female	%	NT Male	%
Always	6	11	4	11	2	1	0	0
Mostly	19	35	14	37	23	10	5	36
Neutral	13	24	12	32	84	37	3	21
Rarely	14	26	5	13	102	44	6	43
Never	2	4	3	8	19	8	0	0
Total	54		38		230		14	

Table 4.2. I communicate by actions rather than by talking.

Have The Numbers Gone Nuts?

Interviews with autistic participants revealed that simply being together without conversing was enough. They preferred to show affection by doing things rather than offering emotional support. However, to avoid emotional discussions, many said they often chose to distance themselves from their loved ones. On the other hand, NT participants shared that because they wanted more emotional connection than their ASC partner or family members could provide, they often felt abandoned and lonely. Despite this, many autistic participants explained that their lack of involvement didn't mean they didn't love their close ones, it was more about their anxiety around emotional conversations and a lower need to connect deeply through words:

> WALLY   *I don't feel like we have to be conversing, interacting, whatever, all the time. I just want to be in the same house ... I used to like the fact that we could go somewhere and just be in the same space and ... not feel like we had to have frivolous conversation. Just be around each other ... at home and weekends because you know I have a full week and I'm buggered, I need that chill out space at the weekend and she accepts that.*

> STELLA   *Our communication was better before we had a child and while I was in work, partly because we spent less time together.*

> RICHARD   *I do things like, I'll come home and I'll put the kettle on ... I'm not a person to go up and just give [my partner] a hug ... I see if somebody needs help like carrying groceries or something*

A Needs Divide

              like that ... but reading somebody's emotional signs ... it's just not an instantaneous or automatic thing.

SHARON   *I expressed my affection through daily small acts like waking earlier to make coffee and breakfast for him before he went to work ... I also helped him with his work ... as a form of affectionate support and to relieve his work stress so that he was a happier person.*

Most NT participants said they understood that their autistic partner or family members did not have the same need for emotional connection and often struggled with anxiety. However, they still found the lack of emotional conversations, the unresponsiveness during those moments and the resulting lack of emotional closeness to be the hardest parts of their relationships to cope with:

TRACY   *One day he cleaned out the inside of the dishwasher ... and said to me: 'You must be so happy to have a husband like me! There're not many men would do this, you know!' ... I just stood there speechless ... Like I ever cared a hoot about the inside of the dishwasher!*

MAGGIE   *There was no affection, there was no encouragement, there was no hugs, unless you know you've just been chastised ... then you start to say, 'Well am I really worth anything?'... Living with that is really hard, to find an identity for yourself, and self-esteem,*

Have The Numbers Gone Nuts?

yeah and self-confidence. That's what I battle with all the time.

MANDY *We don't say we love each other a lot ... he shows it in different ways so it's not telling me he loves me but then he'll come in with a cup of tea sometimes, so I've taken it as it's his action sometimes, rather than just his words.*

The Need for Solitude's Calmative Effect

Survey results showed that ASC participants often need alone time. Challenges in having emotional conversations and keeping up with the fast pace of social interactions (Figures 4.3 and 4.4), the difficulty in discussing problems (Figure 4.5) and a preference for handling problems on their own (Figure 4.6), seem to contribute to a need for regular periods of solitude.

When asked about the challenge of responding quickly in conversations, 66% of ASC participants said it was always or mostly difficult, whereas 76% of NT participants said they rarely or never struggled with it (Figure 4.3). Interestingly, both groups reported that taking time to process a response in their relationship could lead to arguments. Among ASC participants, 41% said that slow responses could cause disputes and 38% said it only happened occasionally. Similarly, 35% of NT participants agreed that slow replies could spark disagreements, with 36% saying it was an occasional issue (Figure 4.4).

A Needs Divide

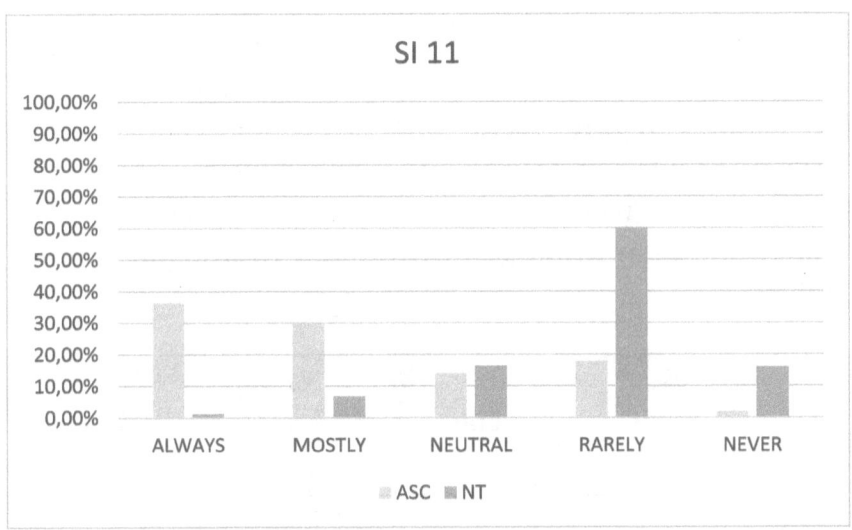

Figure 4.3. SI 11. Responding quickly within conversations is challenging.

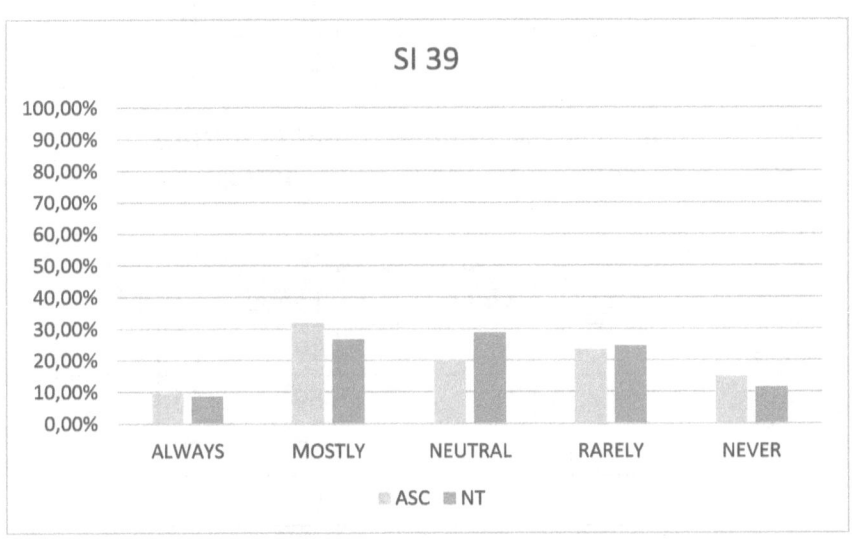

Figure 4.4. SI 39. When I take some time to process a response within conversations it can trigger a dispute.

Have The Numbers Gone Nuts?

Both male and female ASC participants faced similar difficulties with responding quickly, while most NT participants, regardless of gender, did not experience this problem (Table 4.3). Taking into account the sample size for each category, when it came to delayed responses causing disputes, similar responses are found across all participants (Table 4.4).

	ASC Female	%	ASC Male	%	NT Female	%	NT Male	%
Always	28	43	11	27	3	1	0	0
Mostly	16	25	14	35	15	6	2	14
Neutral	8	12	7	17	35	15	6	43
Rarely	11	17	8	20	145	61	6	43
Never	2	3	0	0	40	17	0	0
Total	65		40		238		14	

Table 4.3. Responding quickly within conversations is challenging.

	ASC Female	%	ASC Male	%	NT Female	%	NT Male	%
Always	7	13	2	5	19	8	2	14
Mostly	19	35	11	29	59	26	6	43
Neutral	10	19	9	24	67	29	3	21
Rarely	9	17	12	32	57	25	3	21
Never	9	17	4	11	28	12	0	0
Total	54		38		230		14	

Table 4.4. When I take some time to process a response within conversations it can trigger a dispute.

A Needs Divide

Autistic respondents showed some mixed feelings when asked about discussing problems. About 44% said they preferred to talk about problems, 27% did not want to and 28% were neutral on the matter (Figure 4.5). On the other hand, the majority of NT respondents (77%) preferred to discuss their problems rather than just 'move on'.

There was also a clear difference in how each group preferred to solve problems. A large majority of ASC respondents (79%) said they preferred to be alone when working through issues, while 41% of NT respondents agreed with this approach. However, 33% of NT participants disagreed and 26% were neutral (Figure 4.6).

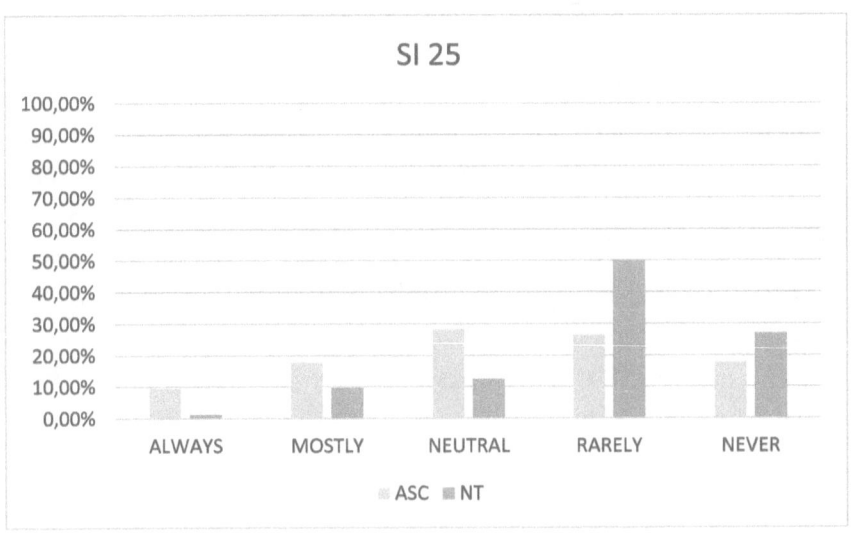

Figure 4.5. SI 25. I believe it is best to 'get over it' and move on rather than discuss problems.

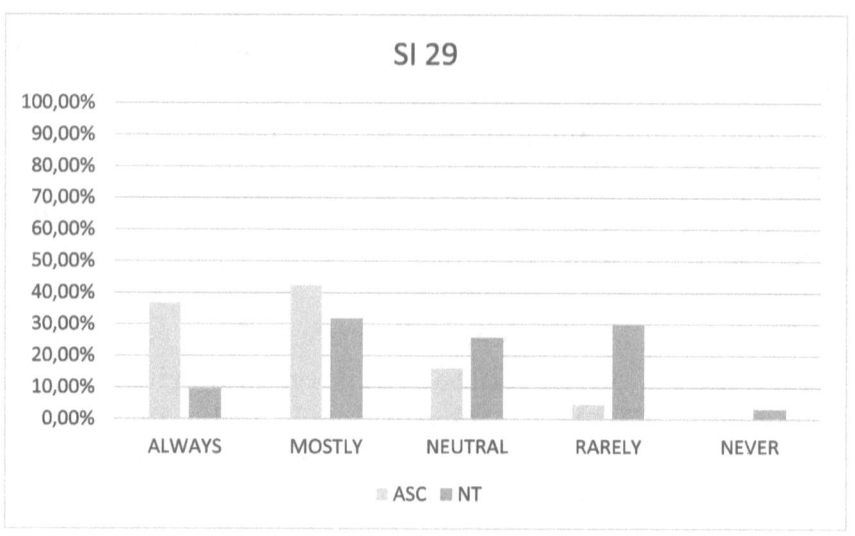

Figure 4.6. SI 29. Problems are best solved by thinking them through privately before deciding on a plan of action.

Although the results in table 4.5 shows that ASC females, NT females and NT males are mainly in agreement with discussing problems, their interviews told a different story. The majority of respondents concurred with the statement that thinking through a problem privately is best, however it is worth noting that 30% of NT females and 29% of NT males indicated that this is not always the best method (Table 4.6).

A Needs Divide

	ASC Female	%	ASC Male	%	NT Female	%	NT Male	%
Always	4	6	6	15	3	1	0	0
Mostly	10	15	9	23	23	10	1	7
Neutral	17	26	12	31	25	11	6	43
Rarely	21	32	6	15	119	51	5	36
Never	13	20	6	15	65	28	2	14
Total	65		39		235		14	

Table 4.5. I believe it is best to 'get over it' and move on rather than discuss problems.

	ASC Female	%	ASC Male	%	NT Female	%	NT Male	%
Always	28	43	9	23	22	9	2	14
Mostly	26	40	19	49	73	31	6	43
Neutral	10	15	7	18	62	26	2	14
Rarely	1	2	4	10	70	30	4	29
Never	0	0	0	0	8	3	0	0
Total	65		39		235		14	

Table 4.6. Problems are best solved by thinking them through privately before deciding on a plan of action.

For many participants with ASC, connecting and communicating with others was not a priority, and spending time alone was preferred:

STELLA   *Sometimes I just need to be left alone and it would be the greatest way of showing he cares ... I feel threatened by his voice,*

Have The Numbers Gone Nuts?

facial expression and other non-verbal communication ... I'm scared of strong emotions.

RACHELLE *What's going on in my own head is far more important than what is coming out of other people's mouths.*

SANDRA *If he's trying to maybe be emotional or affectionate with me and I'm doing something else, it gets that kind of anxious feeling of having to stop what I'm in the middle of and put my focus on what he wants, because in my mind I'm like, 'I'm in the middle of something, I have to finish this and I'm enjoying what I'm doing', so I don't want to stop and do something else.*

Some NT participants mentioned trying to adapt to their partner or family member's need for alone time by seeking connection elsewhere, but they mostly felt like they were missing out on the level of connection they really wanted:

TRACY *The emotional connection I craved seemed to drain my husband, seemed to wear him out, seemed to demand all his energy, so that he had nothing left to give after a few days.*

LUCY *I know they like their solitude, I know you've got to give them their solitude and I don't have an issue with that because I've got a good social life, I've got good friends.*

A Needs Divide

QUINN *I just express how I feel and he either chooses to respond or not ... He would shut down and not say anything and then I just mainly cry ... He doesn't talk. I have to fill up the silence, so I just keep talking.*

The Need for Respite

For autistic people, intense interests and repetitive behaviours can bring a lot of joy and help them cope with daily life. Having a special interest is one of the most common traits in autism. In the past, some autism treatments tried to limit these interests or use them mainly as a reward for good behaviour. However, many autistic individuals see these interests as a key strength and a great way to manage stress. Some turn their passions into successful careers. In interviews, many autistic participants shared that while they knew their focus on special interests sometimes encroached on family time, they usually did not want to change their habits. Instead, they found ways to fit family time around their interests. When conversation becomes personal Stella said:

> *I often feel as if I'm on trial, that I don't know what to say, that my brain becomes paralysed and frozen.*

For that reason, she stated:

> *I would be happiest to spend my days reading and listening to music, without him and our child.*

Whereas Sandra expressed how difficult it was for her to put aside her interests for the sake of others:

Have The Numbers Gone Nuts?

Yeah, I do see that getting very focused and engrossed on something, and then if something else needs to be done ... I get more anxious about having to leave what I'm doing to mind what they need.

The interviews revealed that most of the autistic participants often felt more committed to their special interests than to their relationships. As a result, spending time with their partners usually became less of a priority for them:

RACHELLE *Yes, I'd certainly want to spend a lot more time on my interests than I do on family time.*

SAMUEL *I discovered photography ... It became my obsession ... I get most of the pleasure for my life from that.*

DANIEL *My tendency to spend hours absorbed in computer games, books and other distractions does not pass without comment.*

Murray's perspective revealed that he considered finding a constructive way to confront the matter:

Oh, I think we probably naturally, the Asperger person, can be quite obsessive about things ... I used to gamble ... Not a positive thing to be doing ... once I understood Asperger's, ... okay I'm obsessive, I need to find something positive to be obsessive about.

Many NT participants said that they, and their family members, felt differently about the time spent with special interests. While many understood why their loved one needed

A Needs Divide

a special interest, they struggled with how much time and attention was devoted to it instead of to them. This often led to feelings of resentment, as they felt like they had to compete with the special interest for attention. Laura's disappointment was apparent:

> [He] spends long hours at work ... or internet surfing, all in the name of special interests in news/health. 'Work' becomes the all-purpose reason to be unavailable ... Real reasons — interaction with strangers, going to strange places are hard. He can't say that, so there have to be plausible reasons for being unavailable ... I have to remind myself always, much of this is him, not me, his responsibility not mine. I do what I can to keep us on an even keel but I realise I can't make him happy. Nor can I really create a different relationship.

Many others described how the affection that they sought from their partner/family members also suffered:

> RUTH   Yes, my husband used to spend substantial amounts of time on special interests ... It was horrible ... I felt like I didn't matter, and he didn't want to spend time with our son.
>
> SALLY   He doesn't get it, it takes time away from every part of our relationship, his daughter's relationship.

Left Wanting

It is well known that neurotypical people tend to approach emotional communication and connection differently than autistic people. (Baumeister & Leary, 1995; Grigg, 2012; Marshack, 2009; Mendes, 2015; Simone, 2009). Research has shown that NT individuals often rely on emotional and personal conversations to form the close relationships they need (Ariyo & Mgbeokwii, 2019; Pasch et al., 1997). Survey and interview results confirmed that NT participants try to connect with their autistic partners or family members by seeking meaningful conversations, emotional support and personal interactions.

A Need for Affectionate Dialogue

The survey responses to SI 1, SI 2, SI 9 and SI 43 (Figures 4.7 to 4.9), together with SI 22 and SI 24 in Chapter 2 (Figures 2.6 and 2.7) show that NT and ASC participants react very differently when it comes to affectionate conversations. The data highlights that these differences affect how much each group is willing to engage in deep, expressive conversations. Interviews further revealed that NT participants often felt their need for warm, affectionate communication wasn't fully met in their relationships.

Even though NT and ASC respondents mostly agreed on what makes communication effective, this did not always result in actual effective communication between them. For example, 99% NT and 83% ASC respondents agreed that taking turns leads to better communication (Figure 4.7). Similarly, 98% NT and 71% ASC respondents agreed that actively participating in conversations improves communications (Figure 4.8).

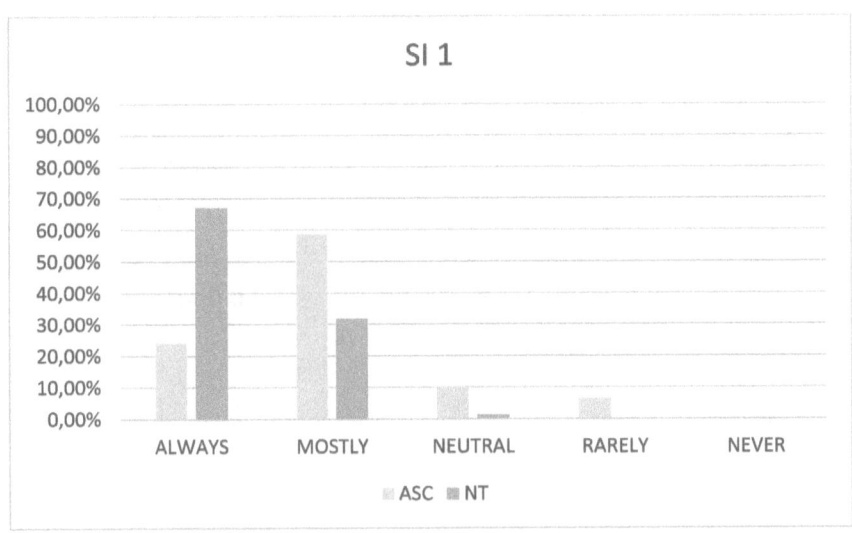

Figure 4.7. SI 1. Taking turns in talking can make communication more effective.

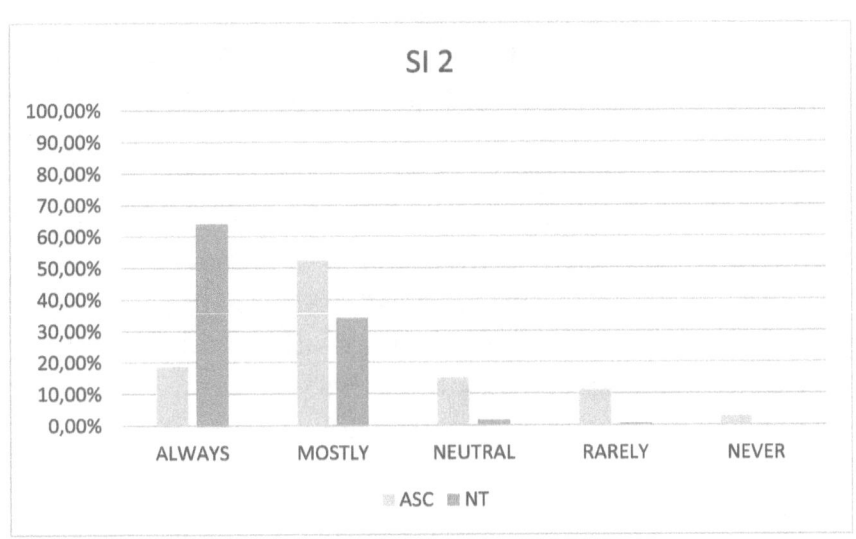

Figure 4.8. SI 2. In order to acknowledge what a person is saying it is important to give eye contact, nod and/ or make comments, such as 'I see', 'mmm' or 'yes'.

Have The Numbers Gone Nuts?

However, while ASC and NT respondents agreed with each other on the survey, their interviews revealed that understanding these communication principles did not necessarily lead to acting on them. Georgia (NT) said:

That's the problem with that reciprocal relationship that most of us ... are searching for, but an Asperger person doesn't seem to be able to give or understand.

Likewise, Terry (ASC) revealed that he could not apply his understanding to his relationship:

Kim would like to have more communication interaction with me ... rather than just sit and listen.

Another well-known difference between NT and ASC people is how they perceive non-verbal communication, and this study highlighted that difference. According to the survey, 96% of NT respondents agreed that body language helps convey meaning, but 42% of ASC respondents disagreed (Figure 4.9). Interviews corroborated these survey results, confirming each group's different viewpoints. The survey also showed that NT respondents placed more importance on both verbal and non-verbal communication, with 94% saying they participated in conversations this way, compared to just 49% of ASC respondents (Figure 4.10).

A Needs Divide

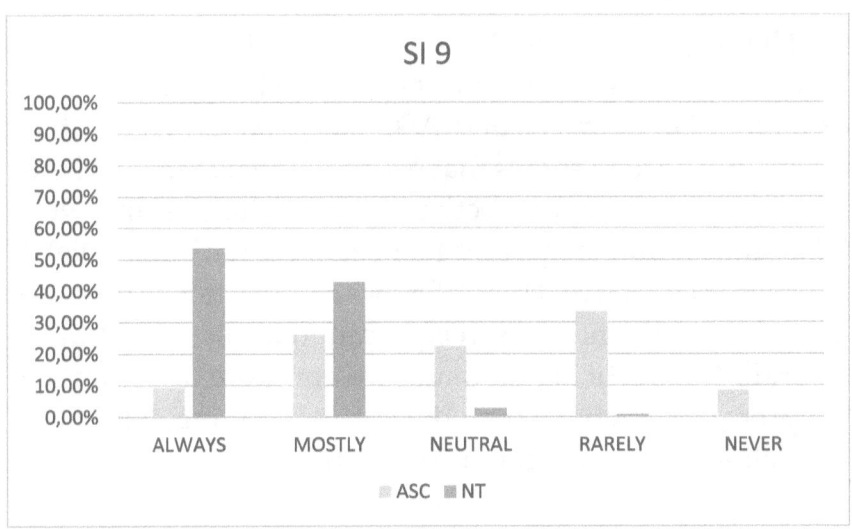

Figure 4.9. SI 9. Attending to a speaker's body language can make it easier to decipher the real meaning of what she/he is talking about.

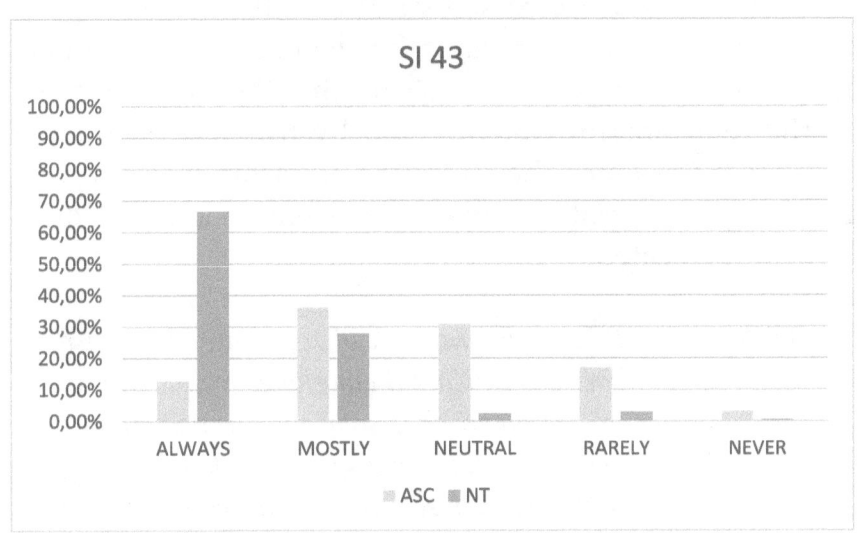

Figure 4.10. SI 43. I participate in conversations both verbally and non-verbally (for example, by nodding or gesturing).

Have The Numbers Gone Nuts?

The responses to SI 22 and SI 24 in Chapter 2 (Figures 2.6 and 2.7), along with interview feedback, highlight a clear difference between NT and ASC participants' views about affection. The data shows that NT individuals often feel they aren't getting enough affection in their relationships, while ASC individuals generally feel satisfied with the level of affection they receive. This difference also extends to how each group views the need for reciprocation in these exchanges. Overall, NT participants tend to want more affection and reciprocal interactions than they were receiving, while ASC participants did not seem to feel the same need for any increase.

A Need for Connectedness

While NT participants recognised that their partner or family members either did not enjoy or were not good at deep, meaningful conversations, they still wished for them to understand how important they were to their emotional needs. Many NT participants said that their commitment to the relationship was affected by this lack of deeper conversations since the support and effort they put into fostering emotional closeness often went unacknowledged or unreciprocated:

> TRACY *Reactions and lack of reaction also set up barriers which kill emotional reciprocity. If, when you speak to someone, the person does and says nothing, one gradually stops speaking to that person, so: no emotional connection. If he regularly says things which hurt you, you progressively pull back emotionally and get your emotional input elsewhere.*

A Needs Divide

NORA *Well obviously we've both got different emotional needs and I probably have a higher need for emotional sort of intimacy and responsivity and desire to sort of be seen by my partner. He's happy with how things are because he doesn't need as much on that scale and basically there's a disparity there which means I'm lumped with how it is.*

Studies have confirmed that partners' responsive behaviours across a wide range of experiences predict greater personal and relationship wellbeing (Finkel et al., 2017). Therefore, unresponsiveness and affectionate connection deficiencies are not representative of what would be considered 'normal' for close relationships. Dianne summarised the general NT sentiment:

I actually sit on the train and look at couples that sit together on the train and converse with one another and think 'Gee, I wish my relationship was like that.' ... Nothing is kind of natural if you like. Nothing comes because it's fun. There is no fun in the relationship. It is always tentative. Jim is always very defensive ... there is no spontaneity. There is no ... hug as you walk in the door ... or a bit of fun, or a bit of laughter. Not even normal conversation ... Jim will tell me three days later something that's happened, and yet we will sit at the dinner table just about every night with nothing to say ... and the couple will sit and just even the way they look at one another. You think, 'Oh wouldn't that be nice if he just looked at you one day like you are the best thing since sliced bread.' ... probably that's what I miss the most. The natural things that I would see as naturally occurring, you know, in a relationship.

Have The Numbers Gone Nuts?

However, many ASC participants shared that they either did not feel comfortable or simply did not want to engage in this affectionate, back-and-forth type of conversation. Some said they often did not realise when their partner or family members needed that kind of interaction or connection. Even if they did notice, some were not sure how to respond, while others admitted they sometimes felt frustrated or annoyed when their partner or family members tried to push or prompt them into having these conversations:

RICHARD *But reading somebody's emotional signs ... the light bulb doesn't go off in my head.*

EDITH *I can't construct those conversations as well as I'd like ... Never guaranteed to be able to do it ... I can't read the body language well enough to know.*

WALLY *Clearly, I'm not able to ... I think she has an expectation ... some kind of emotional support that I may even not recognise the need to give at the time she needs it, so yeah, it's a bit of a minefield.*

SAMUEL *[My partner] really needs to hear people's opinions about things to make her feel that she's doing the right thing ... debrief about her day which was something I always found kind of annoying.*

Yet, Matt (ASC) shared that even though it was difficult for him, he recognised the importance of working at reciprocal interaction and connection for the sake of the relationship:

A Needs Divide

Any change in a relationship is really by invitation, I invite you to meet my needs ... and without that kind of reciprocal meeting of invitations, the relationship does in fact suffer because it doesn't change, and the needs aren't met.

A Need for Emotional Support

When it comes to emotional support, the survey and interview data highlight another key difference between NT and ASC participants. The NT participants wanted companionship that included warmth, closeness and chances to have deep, meaningful conversations about personal and relationship issues. On the other hand, ASC participants, while logically understanding the importance of these elements in relationships, preferred much less of them. Instead, they desired more time for solitude and seclusion, as discussed previously. Even though SI 10 (Figure 2.4 in Chapter 2) shows that most participants from both groups believed meaningful conversations were important for close connections, 53% of ASC participants and 82% of NT participants felt they did not connect with their partner or family members during these important conversations (Figure 4.11).

Have The Numbers Gone Nuts?

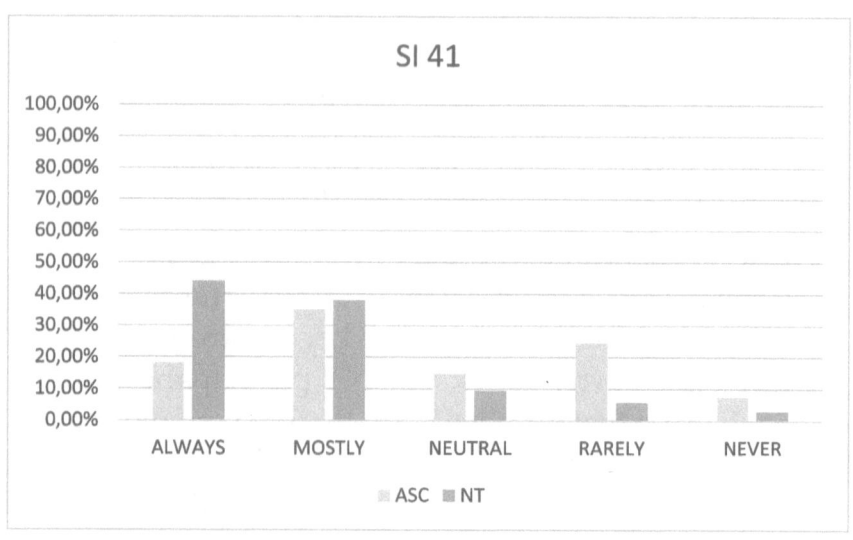

Figure 4.11. SI 41. I feel that we do not connect (that is, we are not 'on the same page') when attempting to have important conversations.

Both ASC and NT males and females all agreed that they were not 'on the same page' when attempting important conversations (Table 4.7).

	ASC Female	%	ASC Male	%	NT Female	%	NT Male	%
Always	10	19	7	18	105	45	3	21
Mostly	15	28	18	47	85	37	8	57
Neutral	9	17	4	11	23	10	0	0
Rarely	15	29	8	21	12	5	2	14
Never	5	9	1	3	6	3	1	7
Total	54		38		231		14	

Table 4.7. I feel that we do not connect (that is, we are not 'on the same page') when attempting to have important conversations.

A Needs Divide

Unravelling Households

It was discovered that many relationships started to fall apart due to these ongoing differences. Most NT participants shared that the lack of the companionship they needed caused their relationship to break down for them. Some became resigned to the disconnect, while others felt sadness that pushed them to seek companionship outside of the relationship. A few tried to understand the difficulties and accept the situation as it was. It became clear from the interviews that all NT participants felt some level of disconnection from their partner or family members. For most, the absence of the close companionship they longed for but could not resolve led to feelings of frustration and discontentment:

> QUINN *I would ask something ... and he would never respond ... I would go to bed crying ... he never came and held me. He never came to ask what was wrong ... I can't get over the hurt ... He can't connect with me emotionally to give me the assurance that I need ... so I need to get over it on my own and I have no idea how to do that.*

> MAGGIE *It's just a nightmare and I battle with the lack of connection, especially with [my daughter]. I battle with being able to hug her ... that sensory stuff ... and I get that ... I will live with the pain of that, but if I could have a more of an emotional connection with her that would be fine.*

Have The Numbers Gone Nuts?

> LAURA   *He does not seem to want or solicit greater connection except that he does sometimes seem to seek out my presence ... I wish he paid me more attention, noticed me more, shared more of his inner life with me ... [I] often feel we just live two parallel lives.*

In contrast, many ASC participants revealed that they did not appreciate the requirement placed on them to talk and connect to the satisfaction of their partner/family members:

> SHARON   *I was thinking about obligations to explain myself repeatedly over the same matter. That happened in the relationship and I was not pleased to have to do that.*

> TERRY   *I suppose that's probably about 1 in 10 that we manage to talk things through to Kim's satisfaction.*

> RACHELLE   *We just go through our daily lives and we don't actually stop and connect.*

A Notable Famine

These relationships were found to experience a notable absence of emotional connection and intimacy. SI 34 (Figure 2.5 in Chapter 2) shows that deep and meaningful conversations often do not take place, and Figures 4.12 to 4.15 in this chapter, highlight several key elements of conversation that are missing in neurodiverse relationships when it comes to creating closeness between people.

A Needs Divide

While most respondents from both ASC and NT groups agreed that using 'I' statements is the best way to express feelings, with 85% of NT and 67% of ASC respondents supporting this (Figure 4.12), each group had different viewpoints when it came to using these statements to express love or care. For example, 53% of NT participants said they would like to regularly hear affectionate affirmations like 'I love you' or 'I care' (Figure 4.13), and 70% felt that these affirmations are essential in close relationships. On the other hand, 43% of ASC respondents said they would like to receive such affirmations, but 37% felt that giving them was not really necessary. So, while many ASC participants seem to want to receive these affirmations (according to responses to SI 12; Figure 4.13), a good portion of them also think that giving them is not that important (as shown by responses to SI 17; Figure 4.14).

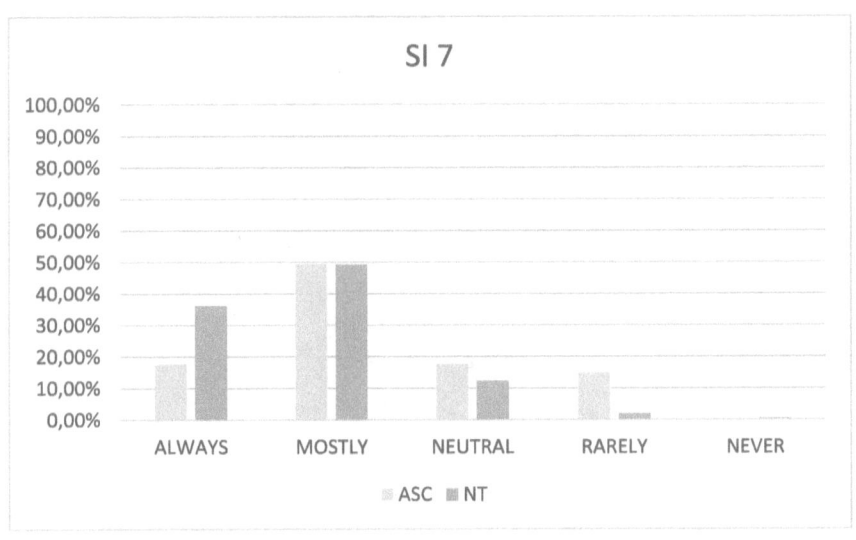

Figure 4.12. SI 7. The best way to communicate my feelings is to use 'I' statements, such as, 'I think...', 'I feel...', 'I need...'.

Have The Numbers Gone Nuts?

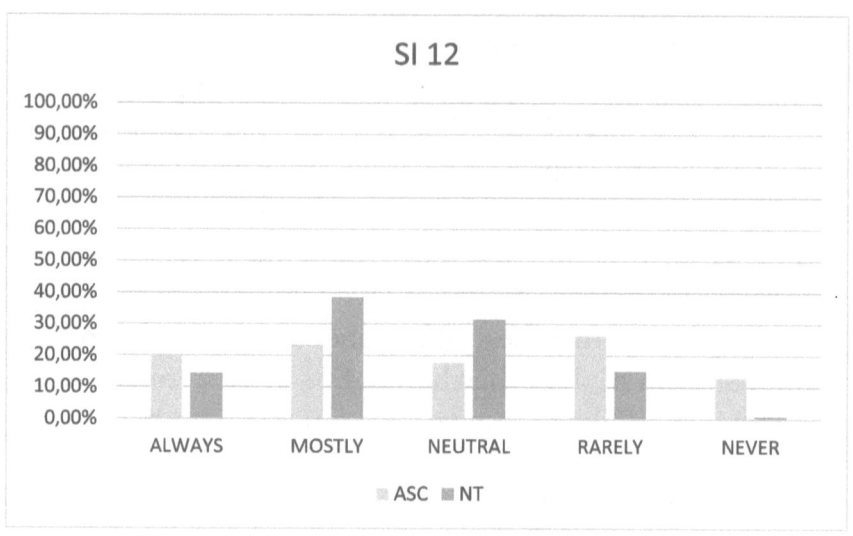

Figure 4.13. SI 12. I need to receive frequent affirmations, such as 'I love you', 'I care' or 'I understand'.

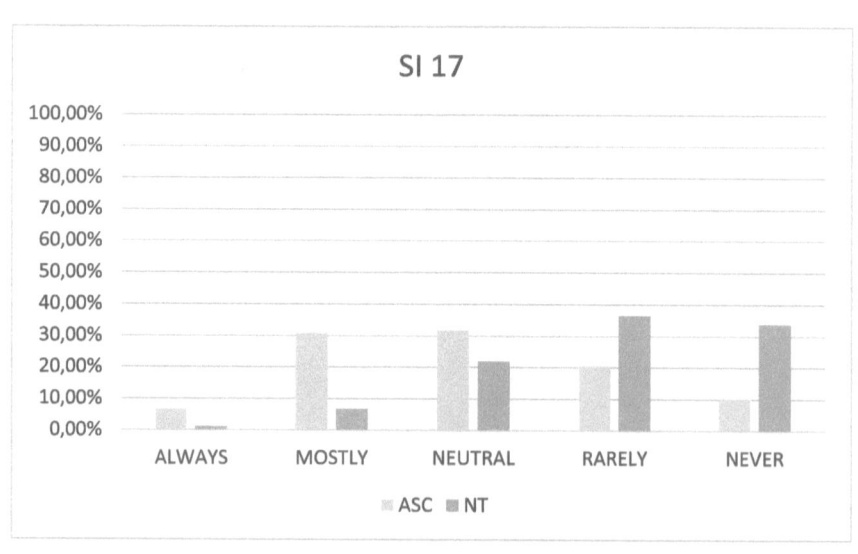

Figure 4.14. SI 17. Saying things like 'I love you', 'I care' or 'I understand' on a regular basis is not necessary.

A Needs Divide

Although most respondents (81% of NT and 52% of ASC) agreed that their relationship would improve if they had more meaningful conversations (Figure 4.15), responses to SI 34 in Chapter 2 (Figure 2.5) show that both groups said these types of conversations rarely happen in their relationships. When a lack of meaningful conversations combines with an absence of regular affectionate affirmations (Figure 4.14), it creates a barrier to building the emotional closeness needed for strong connections. Even though ASC respondents recognised the importance of meaningful conversations (Figure 4.15), they did not seem to follow through on that understanding.

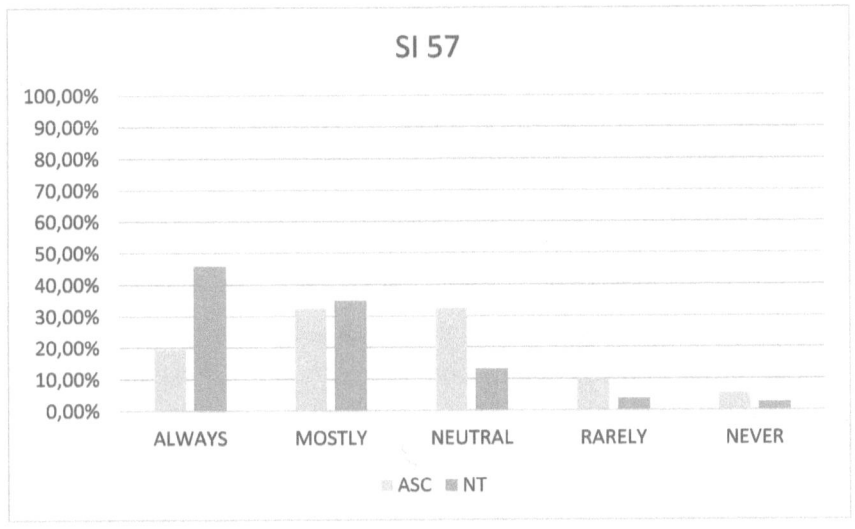

Figure 4.15. SI 57. Our relationship would improve if we had deeper, more meaningful conversations.

Naturally, most ASC and NT males and females all agreed that their relationship would improve if they had deeper, more meaningful conversations (Table 4.8).

Have The Numbers Gone Nuts?

	ASC Female	%	ASC Male	%	NT Female	%	NT Male	%
Always	11	21	6	16	103	44	3	21
Mostly	14	27	16	42	74	31	8	57
Neutral	19	37	11	29	43	18	3	21
Rarely	5	10	4	11	11	5	0	0
Never	3	6	1	3	5	2	0	0
Total	52		38		236		14	

Table 4.8. Our relationship would improve if we had deeper, more meaningful conversations.

While the results shown in Table 4.8 revealed both groups agree that their relationships would improve with deeper, more meaningful conversations, survey text responses show a different story. An NT survey respondent revealed the frustration of this lack of emotional connection:

My experience of the relationship would be better if I felt connected with my ... partner and received acknowledgements that we exist as a couple. Communication is almost always frustrating.

In contrast, a respondent with ASC confirmed that he did not have the same need for connection that his wife did:

I don't feel the need to connect emotionally in the way [my wife] does. Only in the past 5 years have I understood that I have ASD, but in hindsight can see relationship difficulties throughout our marriage that it has impacted and exacerbated.

A Needs Divide

The interview data also highlighted that NT respondents' need for deep, expressive conversations, affectionate exchanges and intimate communication was often left unmet. All NT participants in the study shared that, while they felt their partner's or family members' needs were being met to some degree, their own needs were left completely unmet. The absence of the expected warmth and intimacy in their relationships made it hard for them to grow closer to their partner or family members. Dianne lamented the lack of closeness in her relationship:

I just tell him he sucks actually. I have done that before ... I have always told him that he has never had to guess about how I feel. I have always told him ... 'Look, this is what I need from you.' And I can think back, way before he was even diagnosed, in our relationship, having those conversations with him, you know. 'I need more of you.' 'You don't give me enough of yourself.' 'You don't talk to me about you.' And being very honest ... I say this is not fair, this is not. I explained that I don't think this is what a relationship should be ... Those things need to happen, and because they don't, this is why we don't have this relationship.

As a result, their unmet needs left the relationship feeling shallow and lacking the depth they were looking for, while superficial exchanges became the norm:

WINNIE *Our day-to-day conversations are superficial. They revolve around chores and how your day has been and it will be very concrete answers like – 'I did x, I ate y for lunch' ... there's no exploration of in-relationship interaction ... It's the realisation that ... things are not going to change, therefore my wanting more affection is only going to make me unhappy … so my response is to go and do more things with other people.*

RENEE   *Conversations tend to be for example 'How did you go at work today?' 'Oh okay.' 'Did you see so and so today?' 'Oh yeah.' 'How are you feeling today?' 'Okay.' … See what I mean? Superficial.*

HOLLY   *If we were to talk about anything very, very superficial. For example, the weather, what the traffic is like, he will volunteer that stuff but if we were to have to talk about the fact that one of the children was having difficulties … it would always be instigated by me.*

On the other hand, participants with ASC, discussed the challenges of being required to offer emotional support, share in meaningful conversation and cultivate intimacy in their relationships:

RICHARD   *It's been a frustrating exercise … I'll give one, or two, word answers, whereas she's looking for … talk[ing] it out a bit more, but as I say that's more … effort on my part.*

RACHELLE   *If I wanted to have fixed it, I would have increased the level of conversation or intimacy … this is the level I'm happy with … No, no I don't think he is happy at all.*

A Needs Divide

Chapter Synopsis

This chapter explained how the different needs of the two groups of participants often clashed with each other. The misaligned needs in each relationship created an imbalance in how affection was expressed and what was considered acceptable by each person. The subsequent imbalances often led to affection and connection problems, creating challenges in relationships. As a result, most neurodiverse relationships became shallow and lacking in depth. The next chapter will explore the beliefs and expectations each have about affection and connection in their relationships.

5

Irreconcilable Differences

'Love means that we can be different,
we can believe different things,
we can value different things.'
Rev Anthony J Tang

Have The Numbers Gone Nuts?

Affection is a fundamental component of relationships. It's the glue that binds people together, providing a sense of emotional connection and intimacy. While it is not uncommon for some people to be less affectionate than others, in relationships when a person needs to experience a different level of affection than what is received, it can lead to feelings of unfairness and frustration.

People in neurodiverse relationships often have different needs for emotional conversation that clash, leading to a gap in how each person expects and expresses love. The result is an imbalance in what each person views as acceptable displays of affection.

Perceptions and Detections

Building on the work of researchers like Aston (2001, 2003), Attwood (2007), Bentley (2007), Bostock-Ling (2017); Bostock-Ling et al. (2012), Grigg (2012), Jacobs (2006), Marshack (2009), Moreno et al. (2012) and Simone (2009), the findings from my studies suggest that affection and connection levels in neurodiverse relationships do not match the typical expectations for close relationships. While it was highlighted that ASC and NT participants have different needs for affection, emotional closeness and responsiveness, it was also highlighted that ASC and NT participants feel very differently about affection and connection. ASC participants felt lower levels were sufficient. NT participants expressed growing dissatisfaction. This imbalance often led to different levels of satisfaction within the relationship.

Irreconcilable Differences

The interviews shed light on how each felt about the lower levels of affection and connection in their relationship. Avoiding emotional interaction often appeared to make things better for ASC participants, while NT individuals felt the opposite. Many NT participants started to question if their ASC partner or family member even cared about them. These doubts, in some cases, also caused concern for a few ASC participants. Murray noted:

> *My wife points out that my ... levels of affection aren't what she would expect normally ... it's very easy for someone to assume that that means that they don't love you as much because you're not as affectionate as they would expect.*

Richard described how his partner questioned his faithfulness as a result of low affection levels:

> *At one time she ... said 'Are you having an affair?'... and I said 'No there's nobody else and I do love you, but I suppose ... I'm just not showing you as much affection as what I did 20 years ago.'*

What emerged from the interviews were that NT participants wanted more affectionate interaction and were concerned with the lack of affection in their relationships. Shirley described her main irritation was that demonstrations of affection she expected usually did not occur:

> *It doesn't come naturally to [my partner] to be warm or affectionate, it's not something that naturally just comes to her head.*

Have The Numbers Gone Nuts?

Likewise, Debra conveyed that she had given up expecting 'loving care' from her son:

> *I find that there is a lot of work on my part to manage the relationship. My son tends to really lack empathy ... I expect a little bit more loving care the way I give to him and I never ever get it, so I've learned to just not expect that thing from him ... He's very stiff, very wooden, doesn't smile, doesn't interact in the conversation very much ... I know he feels love ... but he doesn't know how to integrate the expected expressions of love into a normal kind of interaction with people.*

Similarly, Renee described how her partner was not as affectionate as she would like and was dismayed that he appeared satisfied with the situation:

> *I think he's reasonably happy about it because he doesn't need that level of emotional connection really, or he doesn't appear to ... the fact is I'm his wife, we've been married for coming up 33 years, as long as things are okay in his world, then he thinks that it's okay in my world.*

In a similar vein, Laura shared her view of her relationship:

> *The warmth and affection is a one-way street—I should give it to him, and be content that he solicits/accepts it ... He does not seem to want or solicit greater connection.*

The dwindling level of affection in Sabrina's relationship caused her to become downhearted:

Irreconcilable Differences

The affection stayed for a little while, but then, it just gradually fell off ... and he doesn't seem to be that bothered by it, so that's kind of the sad part.

An Awareness Divide

While the survey responses reveal these different viewpoints about affection and connection (Figures 5.1 to 5.3), they also reveal different viewpoints about a desire for change, with NT participants wanting more affection and connection, while ASC participants were mostly comfortable with the way things were. SI 18 (Figure 5.1) shows the different satisfaction levels between the two groups. Half (50%) of ASC respondents said the emotional connection in their relationships was always or mostly satisfying for them, while a larger portion of NT respondents (69%) said they weren't satisfied. This supports findings reported earlier (SI 24; Figure 2.7 in Chapter 2) that ASC participants were generally satisfied with lower levels of affection and emotional connection, unlike the NT group.

Have The Numbers Gone Nuts?

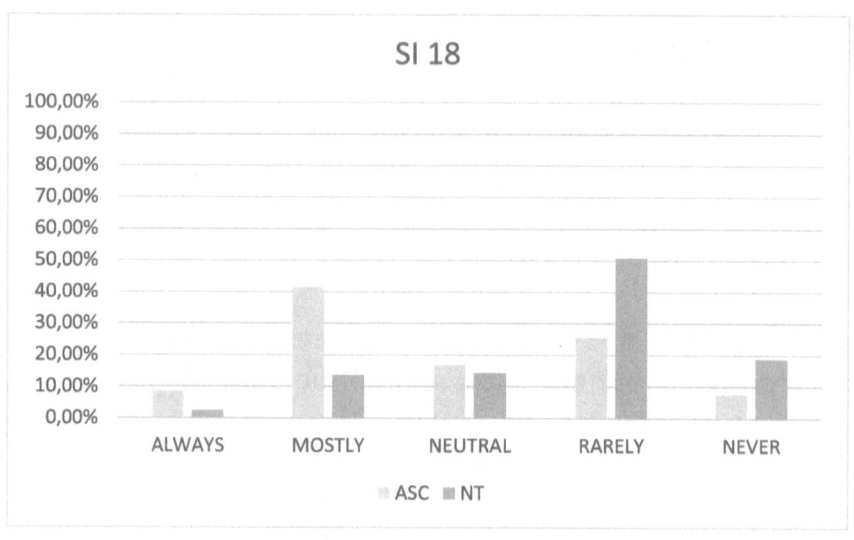

Figure 5.1. SI 18. I am satisfied with our emotional connection.

The results shown in table 5.1 reveal that both male and female ASC participants were mainly satisfied with the amount of emotional connection in their relationships, while over 70% NT females stated that they were rarely or never happy. NT males were somewhat split in their responses (Table 5.1).

	ASC Female	%	ASC Male	%	NT Female	%	NT Male	%
Always	6	9	3	11	6	3	0	0
Mostly	29	54	14	42	29	12	5	36
Neutral	10	15	8	13	32	14	4	29
Rarely	15	23	11	32	122	52	5	36
Never	5	8	3	8	47	20	0	0
Total	65		39		236		14	

Table 5.1. I am satisfied with our emotional connection.

Irreconcilable Differences

Figures 5.2 and 5.3 show another layer to differences in how well each group understood their partner's or family member's satisfaction levels. A significant portion of both groups (42% of ASC and 66% of NT participants), thought their partner or family member was always or mostly satisfied with their emotional connection (Figure 5.2). Similarly, 42% of ASC and 51% of NT participants believed their partner or family member was mostly satisfied with the expressions of affection (Figure 5.3). However, Figure 5.1 indicates that emotional connection was more satisfying for ASC respondents than NT ones, which suggests that many ASC participants may have misjudged how satisfied their partner or family members really were. NT participants, on the other hand, seemed to have a more accurate understanding of their partner's or family member's feelings.

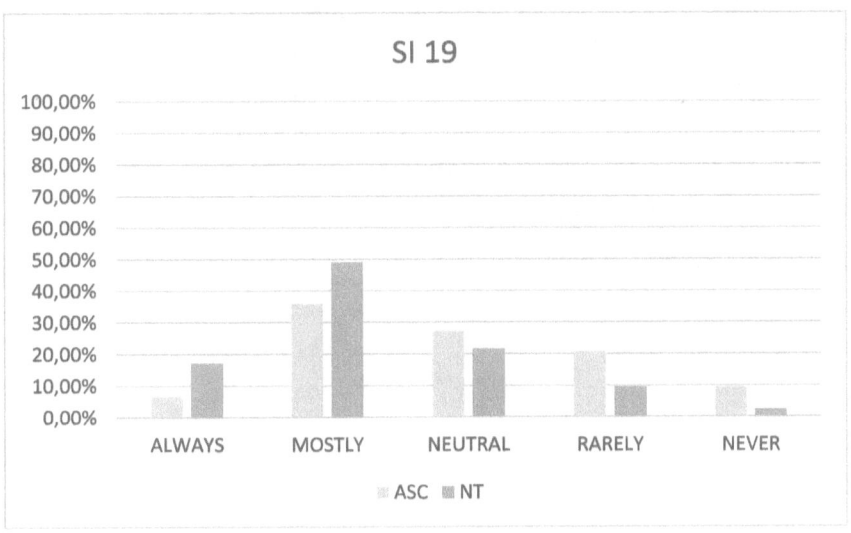

Figure 5.2. SI 19. I think my partner/ family member is satisfied with the amount of emotional connection we share.

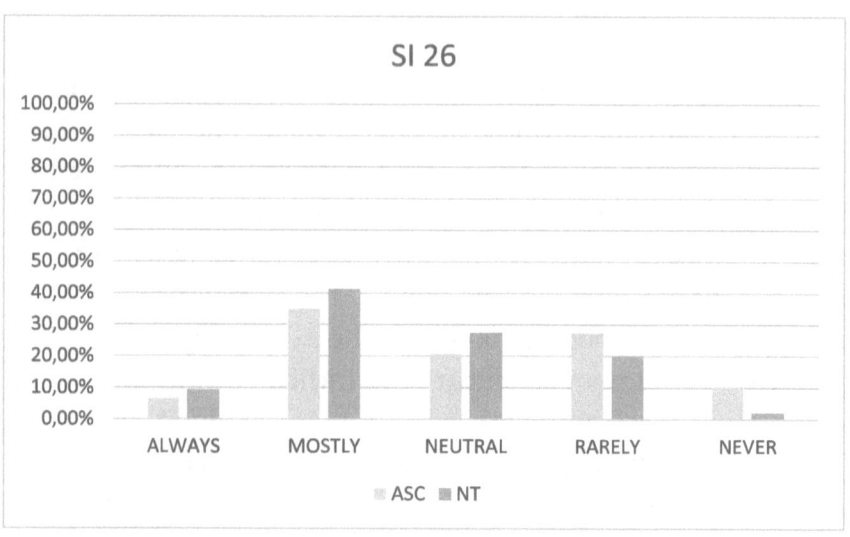

Figure 5.3. SI 26. I think my partner/family member is satisfied with how I express affection toward him/her.

Tables 5.2 and 5.3 suggest some differences among ASC participants. ASC males appeared to be slightly better at gauging their partner's or family member's satisfaction compared to ASC females, or it could be that NT individuals in relationships with ASC females were more satisfied than those with ASC males.

Irreconcilable Differences

	ASC Female	%	ASC Male	%	NT Female	%	NT Male	%
Always	5	8	2	5	43	18	0	0
Mostly	30	46	7	18	117	50	6	43
Neutral	18	28	10	26	50	21	4	29
Rarely	8	12	14	36	20	8	4	29
Never	4	6	6	15	6	3	0	0
Total	65		39		236		14	

Table 5.2. I think my partner/family member is satisfied with the amount of emotional connection we share.

	AS Female	%	AS Male	%	NT Female	%	NT Male	%
Always	6	9	1	3	23	10	0	0
Mostly	29	45	7	18	98	42	5	36
Neutral	13	20	9	23	63	27	5	36
Rarely	13	20	15	38	47	20	3	21
Never	4	6	7	18	4	2	1	7
Total	65		39		235		14	

Table 5.3. I think my partner/family member is satisfied with how I express affection toward him/her.

Confirming the survey data responses, many ASC participants reported that they were reasonably satisfied with the levels of affection within their relationships:

> TOM — *I feel comfortable when I am with Ken and I do not feel lonely. To me that is a satisfactory emotional connection. I don't know how to*

make warm affectionate conversations, but I don't feel anything lacking. Sometimes Ken says our intimacy is lacking.

In contrast, most NT participants showed substantial dissatisfaction. Nora's sarcastic comment revealed her displeasure:

NORA *Well obviously we've both got different emotional needs ... and basically there's a disparity there ... and when I say to him are you happy, he goes 'Yeah, I've got no problems with you. This is great for me, this relationship'. I'm like 'I'm glad you're so happy'.*

SABRINA *I'm the one who's dissatisfied. He's kind of okay because he's getting whatever limited needs that he has met.*

However, Mia's comments illustrated that individual differences still exist. She described how her relationship was distinctively unique to the majority of neurodiverse relationships and, consequently, she appeared to be more satisfied in her relationship than most:

I'm satisfied in our relationship, particularly in regards to understanding the ways that Matt expresses love in that he likes to connect. He likes conversation. He likes to talk about current events and world events and he is a good listener and, yeah. So, I think we do share a good connection in that we talk. We spend time together. It's give and take.

Irreconcilable Differences

Confirming Mia's comments, Matt (ASC) gave his viewpoint on reasons why their satisfaction levels appeared to surpass the average neurodiverse relationship. Also, in regard to Murray's earlier comments, Matt's description gave a possible explanation as to why many NT people experience doubts about their partner/family members' affection:

> *I've had a lot of training with Mia. She's really helped me ... our relationship has improved tremendously ... My natural response is to be Mr Blank Face, Mr Poker Face, and to not interact, not even smile and interestingly ... when I focus on what someone is saying I will lose all expression in the face ... and ... create the impression in the other person's mind that I'm not paying attention to them, when in fact I'm extra paying attention to them ... One of the things Mia did was ... 'Don't do ear only listening' because that's what I do, ear only, and lose other aspects of visual feedback to show that I'm actually paying attention ... but I guess if you don't have that desire to learn or ... willingness to learn, then that itself would be an impediment to learning.*

Hijacked by Roadblocks

The challenge many ASC participants had to communicate with their partners or family members was often made worse by their fears about having conversations which made social interactions stressful for everyone. To cope with their anxiety, many ASC participants chose to avoid conversations altogether as a form of self-protection. While NT participants tried to encourage engagement and help overcome these behaviours, the differing needs between autistic and NT participants made it hard to resolve these communication difficulties, often leaving issues unresolved.

Although most participants, both ASC and NT, felt unresolved issues were a common and ongoing problem, responses to SI 23 about unresolved issues were a bit mixed from the ASC group (Figure 5.4). While 46% said that problems usually or always stay unresolved, 37% said that difficulties rarely or never remain unresolved and 17% were neutral on the issue. In comparison, the majority of NT respondents (79%) felt that problems mostly or always stayed unresolved, while only 11% said that difficulties rarely or never remained unresolved. Just 10% of the NT group were neutral. This difference in perspective seemed to suggest that people with ASC often preferred to avoid dealing with problems rather than resolving them, which could negatively affect relationships. Interviews confirmed these perspectives, revealing that NT participants tended to want to address issues, whereas those with ASC were more likely to avoid them altogether.

Irreconcilable Differences

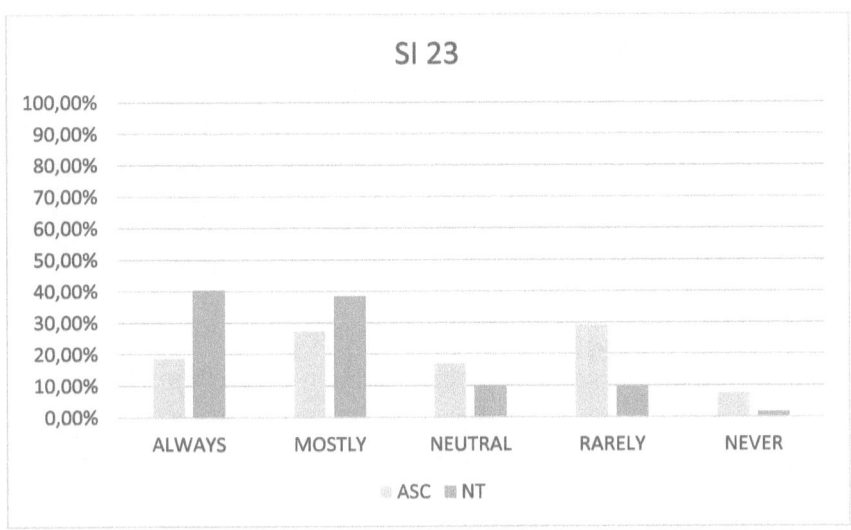

Figure 5.4. SI 23. Difficulties between us remain unresolved.

A survey respondent with ASC shared a noticeably different viewpoint about getting along with others in comparison to the majority of NT respondents:

Now I have had so much therapy and social skills training, that I now go through the motions to get on with people, and wear an invisible mask each day, and do things that aren't authentic, to keep everyone else happy and get ahead in life. Do I believe what I am doing – no. I don't believe it. It is important to other people so I am faking it. It is important to other people to take turns, so I do it. I don't believe it as something important to me, rather it is something important to other people that I fake because I want something out of that other person (information, speed in processing my request, etc.).

Have The Numbers Gone Nuts?

The above statement highlights a common feeling among many ASC participants: while they might intellectually understand how to improve relationships, they may not see personal value in actually making those improvements. On the other hand, a male NT participant shared that, despite wanting to improve his relationship, he struggled to do so, something that many NT participants can relate to:

I am at a loss as to how to improve the relationship. Neither talking it out, or not talking about it, seem to work. It's like, rather than having two individual agendas and one agreed upon cumulative agenda, there is her agenda and - at best - my agenda items are footnotes at the bottom of the page in superscript.

Although many ASC participants described their lack of conversational success, they mainly focused on attempts to escape difficult conversations rather than endeavour to resolve them. Similar to the survey response on the previous page, Daniel described how his partner's prompts had 'trained' him to respond, while still expressing a preference for silence:

Cathy takes care to get my attention and tells me what she has to say clearly. I'm trained to wait for her to solicit response, although I am prone to interrupt. I'm trained too, to answer the question she's asked. Humiliating but effective ... Letting go of frustration helps ... My natural tendency is to fall silent.

Wally lamented that he did not know how to resolve his disagreements with his partner:

Irreconcilable Differences

It's a scary place to go ... so I will avoid ... it's avoiding that confrontation ... and then she says 'you'll go silent for a couple of hours and then ... you'll talk about stuff like as if nothing has happened'... and I'm like 'well what else am I supposed to do?... Maybe it was unresolved but we can't keep hammering away at something until it's resolved because some of these things are unresolvable.

All the NT participants shared that they believed the only way to resolve issues was by encouraging cooperation and addressing uncooperativeness, but they were frustrated with the limited success. Renee explained that in her household, solving problems involved a lot of pre-planning, followed by lists and step-by-step instructions:

I've learnt that problems don't get solved in our relationship by talking about them, they get solved by me thinking about them, thinking through and then going with him 'right this is what we need to do', which takes me back to me being the boss ... which in most relationships that is not how you do things but he was just absolutely okay with that.

Dawn's dissatisfaction was evident by the lack of problem solving:

If we are in a conversation and I said 'I am very unhappy because ...' or 'your behaviour was ...' he will react saying 'well you did such and such'... he never says 'I am unhappy with you because 'or 'I am uncomfortable ...' or 'can we talk about this ...' Never, NEVER.

Quinn reported that her way of dealing with her partner's shutdowns was to 'force' him to be involved by using emails:

Have The Numbers Gone Nuts?

He shuts down ... it's like a defence mechanism ... every time that we have a conversation with some type of disagreement, I think he feels that I'm finding faults ... I kind of force him to be involved. I'll send him emails at work about stuff.

Chapter Synopsis

This chapter revealed that it was the mismatched needs for affection and connection between ASC and NT individuals that was the main reason for frequent feelings of dissatisfaction in these relationships. However, ASC participants generally felt less dissatisfaction than their NT counterparts since they did not need the same amount of affectionate connection and were able to meet their needs in other ways. On the other hand, NT participants often felt unfulfilled, with their need for affection typically going unmet.

The next chapter introduces the second theme, 'prompting triggers' which explores how the unmet needs of NT participants often trigger prompting as a way to initiate communication. It looks at what makes prompting the main strategy in these relationships, the situations that lead to its use, and how this results in many ASC participants developing a reliance on prompts or attempting to avoid the prompts, creating a repeating cycle of prompting behaviours with dependency or avoidance behaviours.

6

A Distinctive Dynamic

'Ultimately the bond of all companionship, whether in marriage or friendship, is conversation.'
Oscar Wilde

Have The Numbers Gone Nuts?

Autistic individuals often process language differently due to differences in brain wiring. They may take longer to understand a statement with a need to take time to think through their response or express their thoughts. Slower-paced responses can make it hard to keep up in fast-paced conversations. When adding sarcasm, humour and abstract ideas into a conversation, it can become even more challenging, leading to misunderstandings. To navigate these challenges, many autistic people use 'scripts' in conversations, borrowing phrases from media or learned scenarios to respond more quickly (Attwood, 2015; Bambara et al., 2021).

The lack of structure in face-to-face conversations can be especially difficult. Additionally, autistic individuals might focus heavily on personal interests, which can come across as monologues, frustrating others. Repetition of words or phrases, along with differences in speech rhythm, tone or volume, can further complicate interactions. They might sound flat, too loud or too quiet, even when their words are meaningful. Missing subtle cues like tone of voice may cause them to interpret figurative statements literally (Attwood, 2015; Nadig et al., 2010; Pelzl et al., 2022). These communication challenges can lead many autistic individuals to avoid deep or emotional conversations. However, these types of exchanges are vital for expressing needs, fostering connection and feeling understood. Meaningful conversations help build emotional intimacy by allowing people to share their thoughts and experiences. Without this connection, relationships may struggle and meeting each other's emotional needs may be difficult.

Due to these conversational difficulties, communication gaps were found to become the pattern in neurodiverse relationships. The data confirmed that NT participants use prompts to overcome these issues and guide conversations, while their autistic partners and family members either rely on, or avoid these prompts. A unique communication cycle shaped by contrasting approaches was found to result as NT participants often resorted to prompting when seeking deeper emotional conversations, addressing a lack of connection, or resolving conflicts and ASC participants often resorted to reliance on or avoidance of these prompts.

Striving for a Remedy

While prompts can help bridge communication differences, sometimes they were found to add to the tension between partners and family members, highlighting the complex dynamics of these relationships. Most NT participants shared that they started using prompts to address the conversational differences or avoidance behaviours of their ASC partners or family members. The goal was to get them more involved, with the hope that this would lead to more affection and connection. However, as discussed earlier in Chapter 2, the responses to SI 24 show that this desired outcome rarely happened. It seemed that people with ASC did not really want these changes (Figure 2.7 in Chapter 2). Instead, the survey found that regularly avoiding communication within their relationships was the most common behaviour among those with ASC. On the other hand, NT individuals rarely did this. In fact, 60% of ASC respondents said their NT partners or family members seldom, if ever, avoided conversations. In contrast, 61% of NT respondents reported that their ASC partner or family member frequently, if not always, avoided conversations (Figure 6.1).

Have The Numbers Gone Nuts?

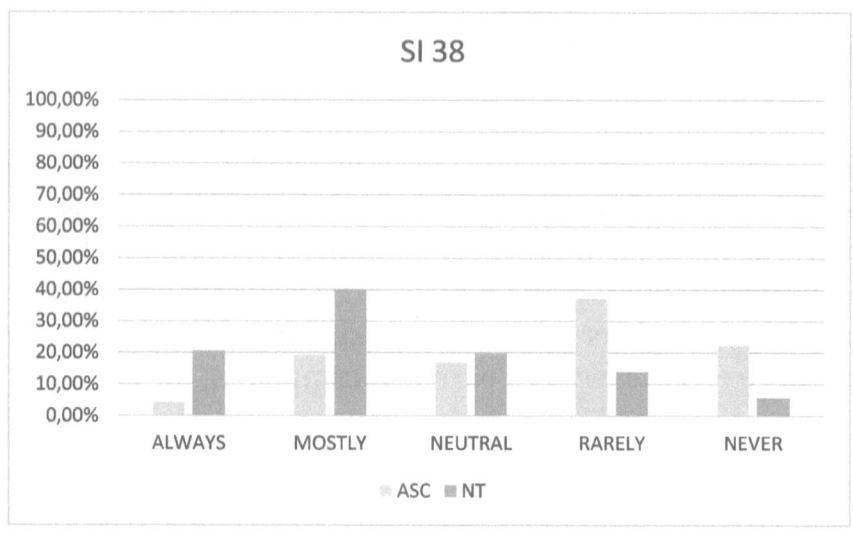

Figure 6.1. SI 38. My partner/family member avoids communicating with me.

This pattern of avoiding conversation can lead to a lack of the warm and affectionate communication previously mentioned (SI 22; Figure 2.6 in Chapter 2). The data also showed that 78% of NT respondents said they frequently or always initiated conversations (Figure 6.2) and 83% said they often took charge in steering conversations (Figure 6.3). However, only 32% of ASC respondents reported frequently or always initiating conversations and 35% said they guided them (Figures 6.2 and 6.3). Interviews with NT participants revealed that they often started prompting conversations because their ASC partners or family members were avoiding them.

The interviews also revealed that conversation avoidance was a key coping strategy used by people with ASC to manage their communication struggles. To deal with this, NT participants often resorted to prompting and guiding conversations as their own coping mechanism. However, this mismatch in coping strategies often led to increased prompting. Interestingly, a few NT respondents admitted that they sometimes avoided conversations too (Figure 6.1). Interviews with these participants explained that they occasionally needed to withdraw from the challenges of difficult conversations with their ASC partner and family members and would stop conversations themselves.

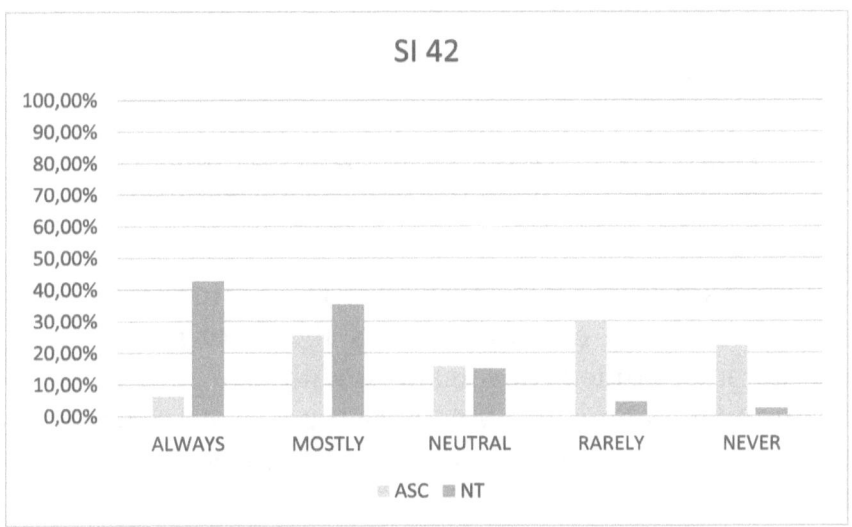

Figure 6.2. SI 42. I have to prompt my partner/ family member to communicate with me.

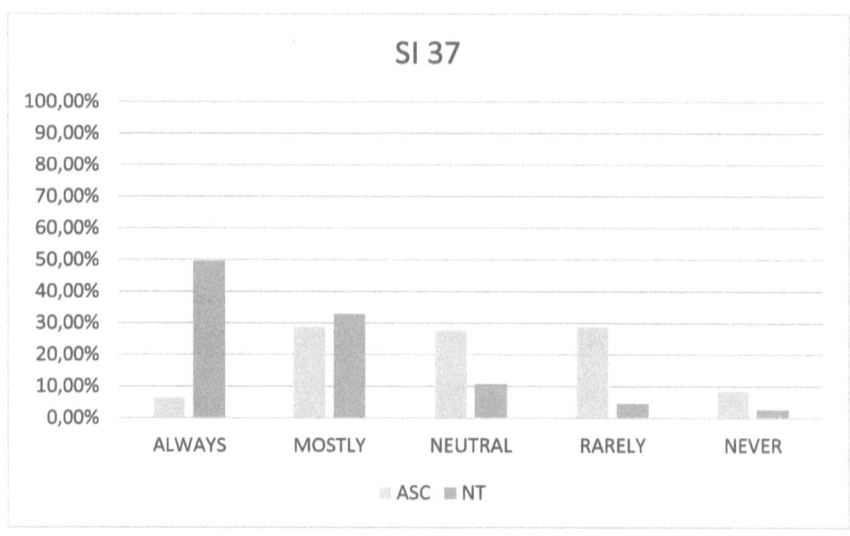

Figure 6.3. SI 37. If I do not direct or guide our conversations, they remain at a superficial level.

Tables 6.1 and 6.2 show that the majority of both male and female NT respondents always or mostly used prompted or guided conversations with their ASC partners or family members whereas these types of strategies were scarcely needed to be used by either male or female ASC respondents.

	ASC Female	%	ASC Male	%	NT Female	%	NT Male	%
Always	5	9	1	3	105	45	3	21
Mostly	18	33	6	16	85	37	8	57
Neutral	9	17	5	13	23	10	0	0
Rarely	14	26	13	34	12	5	2	14
Never	8	15	13	34	6	3	1	7
Total	54		38		231		14	

Table 6.1. I have to prompt my partner/family member to communicate with me.

	ASC Female	%	ASC Male	%	NT Female	%	NT Male	%
Always	5	9	0	0	120	52	1	7
Mostly	18	33	9	24	75	33	5	36
Neutral	15	28	11	29	21	9	5	36
Rarely	13	24	13	34	9	4	2	14
Never	3	6	5	13	5	2	1	7
Total	54		38		235		14	

Table 6.2. If I do not direct or guide our conversations, they remain at a superficial level.

Even though participants with ASC revealed an awareness of the deeper conversations their partner or family members wanted and an awareness that their partner or family members would often try to start or keep conversations going to achieve deeper conversations, many admitted that they didn't always want to join in. Instead, most of the ASC participants seemed to find their loved ones' efforts to connect through conversation unnecessary or even bothersome. Samuel's comments reflected this viewpoint:

> *I would find the prompting about that sort of thing would be annoying ... I don't find it necessary to continue on because her conversations go into what I consider unnecessary detail and repetitiveness ... In a lot of cases I would take our previous discussion as an agreement whereas she would take it as a discussion and ... we still hadn't actually come to a conclusion, according to her. I would find the prompting about that sort of thing would be annoying in a sense in the fact that I thought we'd agreed on something and she's saying no we hadn't.*

Jim's remarks showed that he did not appreciate being prompted to be 'more communicative':

> *'But Jim you've got to be a bit more communicative' ... Like I'm sorry, but I'm no good at interacting with people outside my work environment. Is that a crime? Is that something that I should be ashamed of? I don't think so ... To turn around and say, 'Well you've got to be a bit more considerate, a bit more passionate.' Oh yeah right okay.*

Murray admitted that his emotional responsiveness only occurred when his partner elicits it from him:

> *To be honest it's probably usually reactive, so she'll display affection towards me so I'll try to display affection back. I'm not usually proactive in displaying affection.*

Although Stella indicated that she noticed her partner's attempts to bring about more emotional conversations

A Distinctive Dynamic

between them, she did not respond. Instead, she assumed that his displeasure, and not her lack of response, was the reason for his prompts:

> *I sometimes notice his efforts, but they annoy me, as I either want to be left alone or I need a different way of connection ... Yes, he has prompted conversations, usually straight away, when he was displeased with my behaviour/words.*

Most NT participants said that one of their biggest challenges was not getting the emotional connection they expected in a close relationship. Despite this, many were determined to keep trying to work through these difficulties, especially as they learned more about the ASC condition. Since their partner or family member did not initiate emotional connection and prompting sometimes succeeded, prompting became their main way of trying to connect. All NT participants shared various prompting strategies they used, mostly relying on asking questions, giving instructions or offering explanations. For example, Tracy mentioned that she gave instructions to get affection and connection, but even though this worked at first, her partner would soon return to his 'old ways' and she'd have to give more instructions again:

> *I have tried time and time again ... Like, I would tell him something and he would do it for two days. Then it was back to the old routine.*

Ruth shared how she only achieved connection with her ASC husband when she prompted with questions:

> *With prompting, my husband tries to put forth the effort to connect with me, not just share information. I am the one*

Have The Numbers Gone Nuts?

who has to ask him questions in an effort to connect. He doesn't go out of his way to connect with me.

Dianne said that she used a range of non-verbal methods to prompt such as lists:

If things need to be done, I write a list of tasks to be done cause, they are not good planners, and if I don't put a list down to go, 'These things need to be done', he would just sort of kind of fart around for the day.

Shirley described how she was required to find the 'right' questions to get answers:

In order for me to get the information I want, I have to be very specific about how I prompt her with my questions to give me the information. If I don't ask the right questions then I won't get that information voluntarily. So, she's not going to sit on the couch and say 'Oh I had a really hard client today that came in and this is what happened' ... If I said to her when she got home 'How was your day? Did you have any rough clients, or did you have any hard clients?' Then the story will come out. So, sometimes with Jill it's like getting blood from a stone ... If I don't ask the right question, I won't get the information spontaneously which is sometimes extremely frustrating that I have to try and guess what the questions are, but yeah, she finds it really hard to enter spontaneous conversations about her day so yes, I do have to prompt a lot.

Kay used a pattern of positive reminders:

'Did you understand what I was feeling or what I meant before? Or how that went?' So it is constantly going back

A Distinctive Dynamic

and reminding and reminding this is what happened. This is how I felt. This is what I need. Again. And can we move forward and have an agreed way forward? And consistently going back to that. Going back to that until it is almost like a habit.

Alex prompted with positive justifications to increase Mary's involvement:

Well, the communication I guess, it is not me trying to talk her into it but maybe trying to outline the benefits of maybe doing it, whether it be a social thing with friends, or just going to someone's house for dinner where she doesn't want to. And usually, ... she walks away and she is knackered but she goes 'Oh wow, I had a really good time' ... And that is sort of what I guess I am trying to communicate with her is like 'Do you remember the last time where, as much as you hate the thought of it before we are there, but once you are there you seem to sort of, click and enjoy yourself?' ... So that's about it. It is more trying to outline the benefits of doing something like that. What she will get out of it.

Dawn said that asking questions was her way to get the information she required:

I've learnt not to expect normal communication about information. I have to ask, and I have learnt to accept that I may sound like a nosy nag but if I don't ask, I won't get told.

Seeking Responses

In an effort to meet their emotional needs, prompting was the main strategy that all NT participants used to encourage responsiveness from their autistic partners or family members. However, since meaningful conversation and connection didn't seem to have the same importance for their autistic loved ones, prompting to get more meaningful responses was often not well received by those with ASC.

The data also showed additional explanations for unresponsiveness. According to the answers given to SI 39 (Figure 4.4 in Chapter 4), taking time to respond often caused disagreements for both ASC and NT participants. Likewise, 65% of autistic and 32% of NT respondents said they rarely or never gave expected responses (SI 46; Figure 6.4), combined with 59% of autistic and 71% of NT respondents felt their explanations were frequently overlooked (SI 54; Figure 6.5). These findings indicate that both autistic and NT participants often felt disregarded by their partners or family members and uncertain about how to approach communication. These issues may strengthen the autistic tendency to avoid communicating.

A Distinctive Dynamic

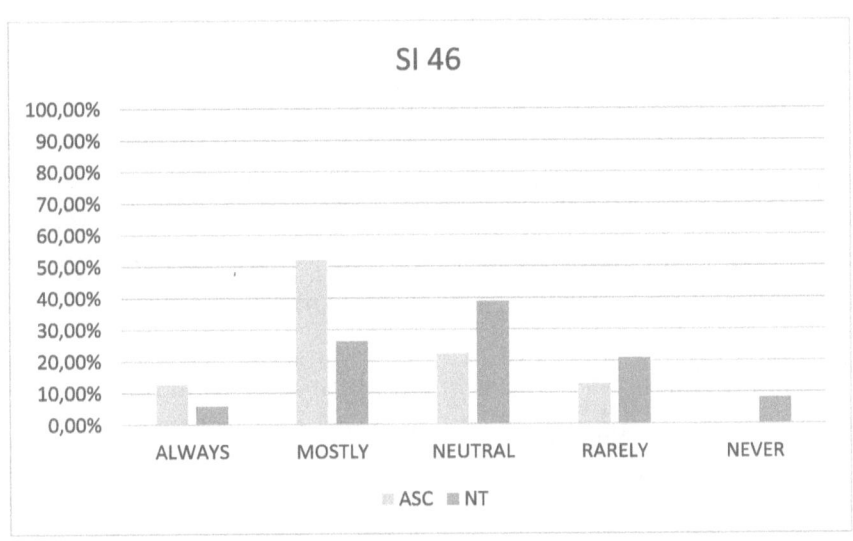

Figure 6.4. SI 46. I do not give the verbal responses my partner/family member expects.

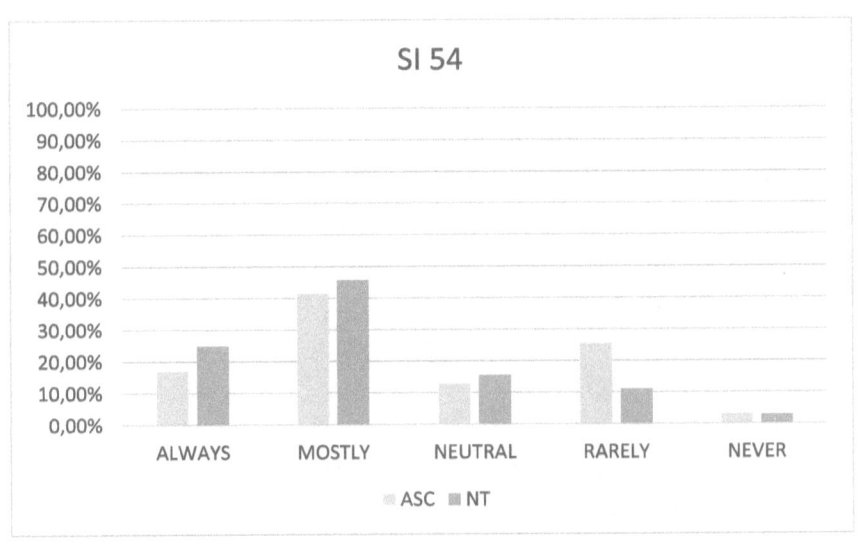

Figure 6.5. SI 54. My explanations are disregarded.

Have The Numbers Gone Nuts?

Regardless of the reasons for unresponsiveness, prompting to improve responsiveness led to mixed results. Most autistic participants acknowledged that their lack of response made it harder for their partner or family members to achieve the desired outcome from prompting. Some even pointed out that their unresponsiveness could sometimes stop the prompting altogether. Sandra's words gave that impression:

He definitely tries to prompt ... because I'm not always positively responding back ... he doesn't really try as much as he used to.

Many neurotypical participants found that dealing with unresponsiveness and the effort needed to get a response was one of the hardest parts of their relationship. Tracy expressed her frustration with how much work it felt like just to get a response:

I have to ask so many questions just to get a very basic piece of information ... I have told him time and time again that I am no wiser after one of his answers than before I asked the question.

Sophie described the effort it took for her to get a response; however, she reported that her efforts were rewarded with some positive outcomes:

I will usually prompt more conversation by initiating with him through questions or asking personal things or things about his interests. I will clearly tell him things like, 'I need you to hold me for a bit', 'I am going to kiss you now', 'Will you please say encouraging or loving things to me', etc. I have to be acutely aware of my own needs and then communicate them to him in a very straightforward manner so he knows

A Distinctive Dynamic

what he needs to do ... Once he gets on a roll, he can chat well but it takes the right prompting to get there.

Struggling to Hold Discussions

Due to its intermittent success, NT participants frequently used prompting strategies to discuss issues, resolve problems and handle conflicts in their relationships. Responses to survey items 14, 25, 29 and 58 highlighted the different ways ASC and NT participants reacted to problem discussions (SI 25; Figure 4.5 and SI 29; Figure 4.6 in Chapter 4, and Figures 6.6 and 6.7). Survey items 47, 51, 53 and 59 provided insight into how each group handled conflict (Figures 6.8 to 6.11).

Responses from survey items 14 and 58 in this chapter (together with 25 and 29 in Chapter 4), showed that autistic respondents generally preferred to avoid problems and conflicts, while NT respondents preferred to face them. A key factor behind this difference was highlighted in SI 14, where 64% of autistic respondents said they didn't like talking through problems, compared to 76% of NT participants who wanted to discuss issues (Figure 6.6). As noted in Chapter 4, responses to SI 25 and SI 29 revealed that autistic individuals preferred to end conversations involving problems and preferred solving them on their own, while NT participants leaned toward discussing and solving issues with their partner or family members (Figures 4.5 and 4.6 in Chapter 4). Responses to SI 58 further showed that 42% of autistic participants wanted to be left alone when upset, whereas 65% of NT respondents preferred to talk through their feelings, even when upset (Figure 6.7). These differences in communication styles played a major role in why prompting was so frequently used.

Have The Numbers Gone Nuts?

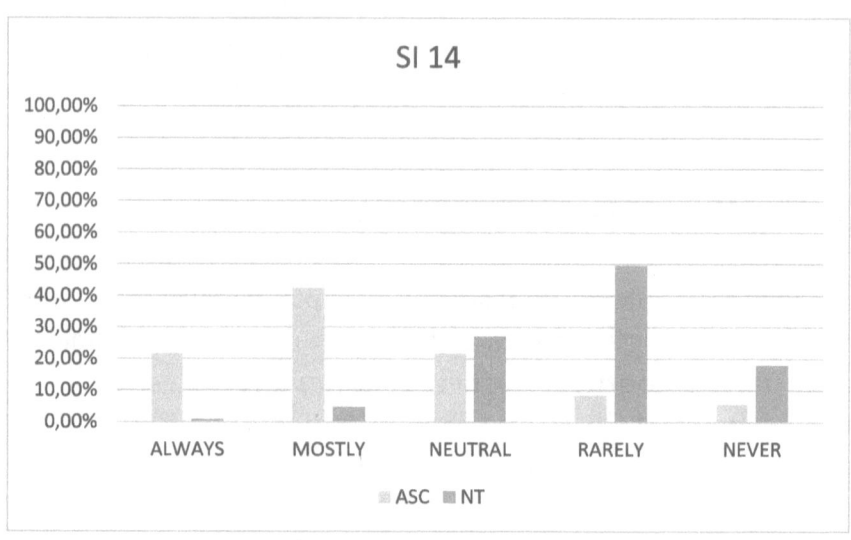

Figure 6.6. SI 14. I don't like being obliged to talk through problems.

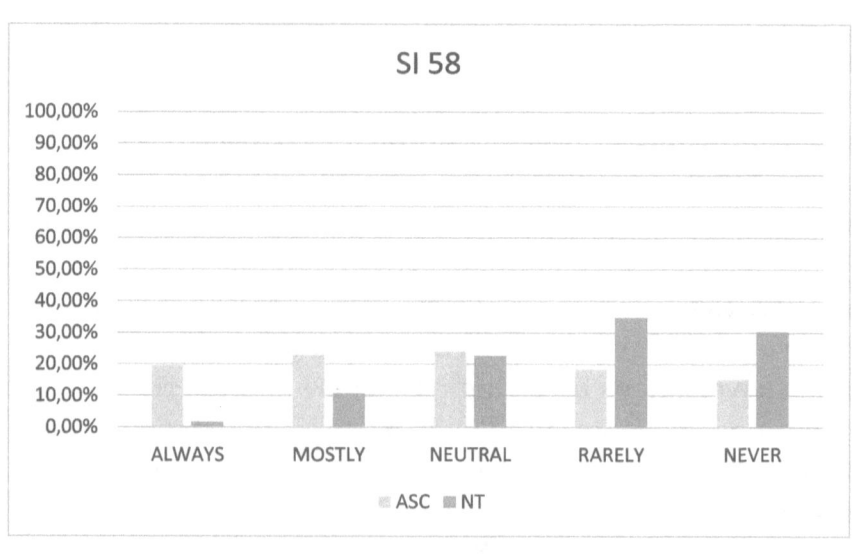

Figure 6.7. SI 58. Our relationship would improve if my partner/family member left me alone to get over it when I am upset, rather than insisting on talking about it.

A Distinctive Dynamic

Surviving Conflict

Survey results from items 47, 51 and 53 (Figures 6.8 to 6.10) showed some key differences in how NT, as opposed to ASC, people respond to conflict. Although NT respondents said that they occasionally avoided dealing with issues by becoming defensive, shutting down or getting verbally aggressive, in contrast, ASC respondents used these behaviours more frequently. Since NT individuals generally want to solve problems (Figure 6.6), the frequent use of avoidance tactics by ASC participants meant that NT respondents often had to step in and prompt them to engage more.

A total of 62% ASC respondents said they always or mostly became defensive, while only 26% of NT respondents said the same (Figure 6.8). When it came to shutting down, 61% of ASC respondents admitted to doing this always or mostly, compared to 33% of NT respondents (Figure 6.9). Additionally, 39% of ASC respondents reported they always or mostly became verbally aggressive, whereas only 17% of NT respondents said the same (Figure 6.10).

Have The Numbers Gone Nuts?

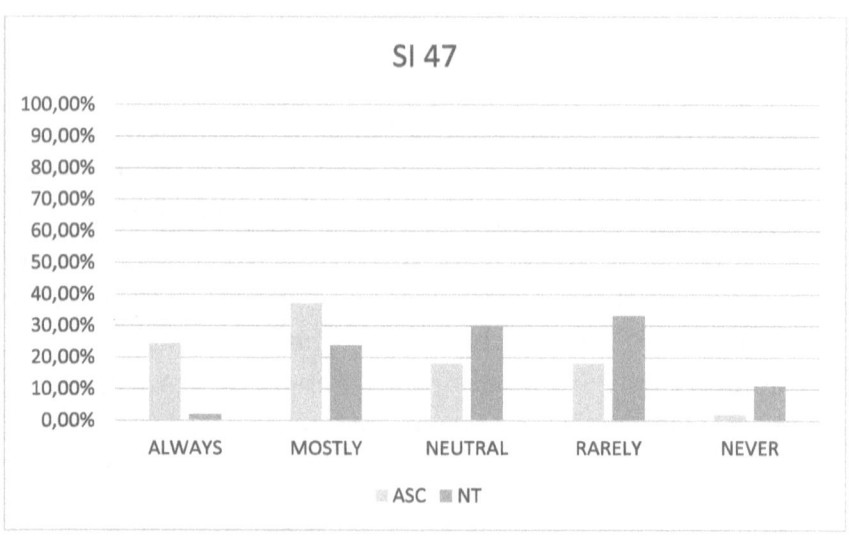

Figure 6.8. SI 47. I can get defensive if I want to stop a conversation.

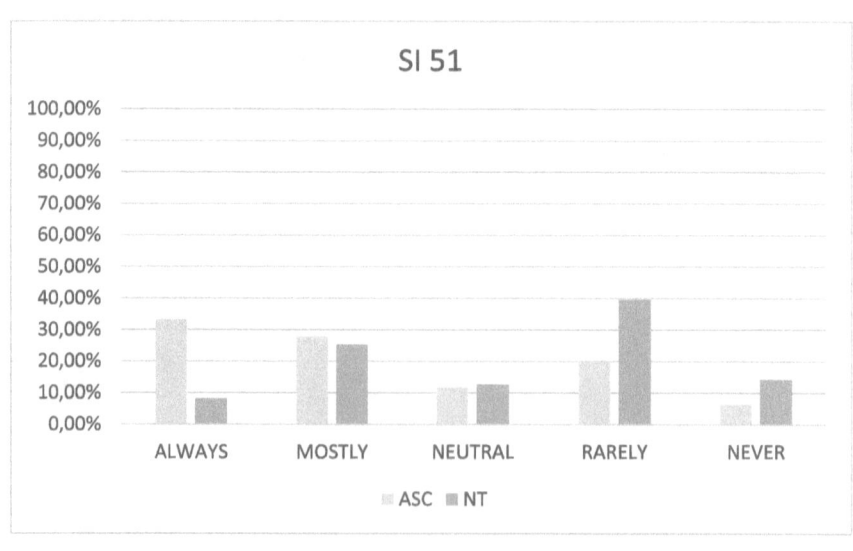

Figure 6.9. SI 51. I shut down (for example, by not responding, or walking away) to end conversations that become difficult.

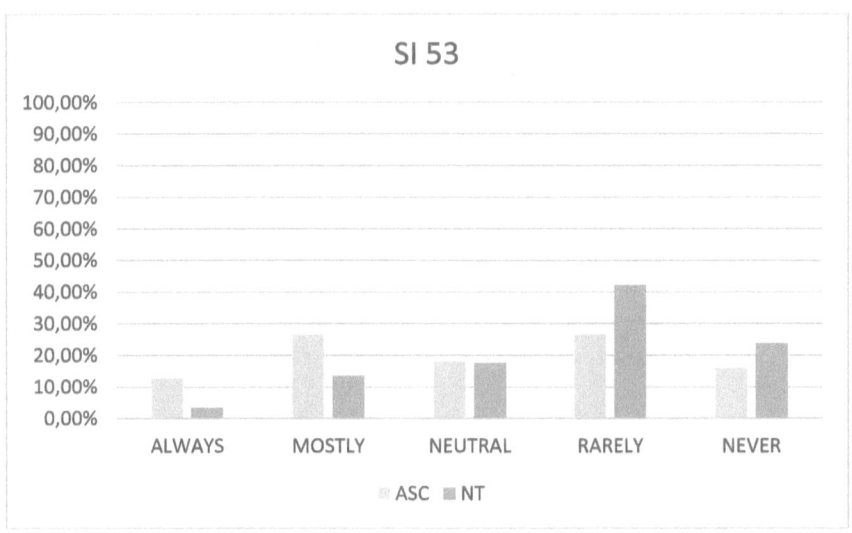

Figure 6.10. SI 53. I can become verbally aggressive to end difficult conversations.

It's interesting to note some inconsistencies between how ASC participants think and how they act when it comes to handling problems in relationships. In the survey, 62% of ASC respondents said that talking through issues with their partner or family member would improve their relationship (SI 59; Figure 6.11). However, during interviews, most of them actually disagreed with this idea and admitted they preferred to avoid discussing problems, even though they knew it may help. In contrast, 77% of NT respondents agreed in both the survey and interviews that talking things out would lead to improvement (SI 59; Figure 6.11).

Have The Numbers Gone Nuts?

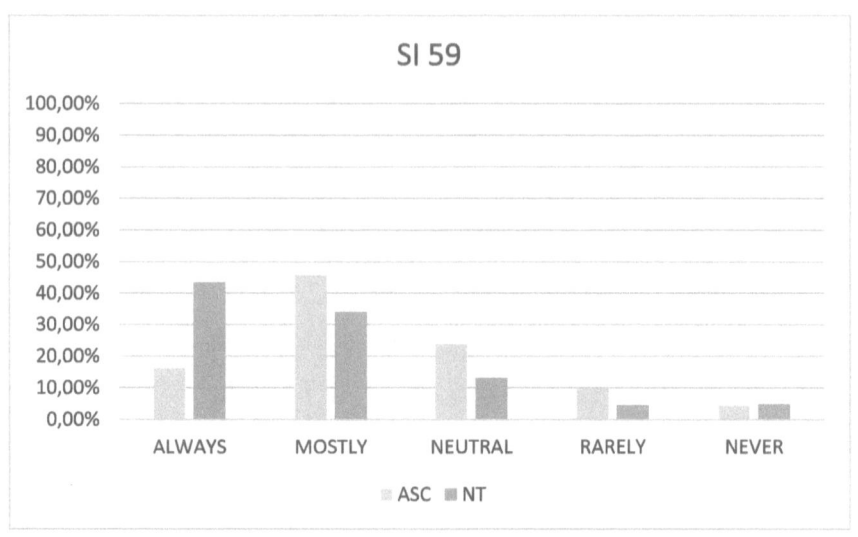

Figure 6.11. SI 59. Our relationship would improve if we still talked about our problems even when it was difficult.

Various unresponsive and avoidant behaviours were discussed by ASC interviewees. Terry conveyed his need to mentally and physically withdraw:

> *I used to just sort of mentally tune out but what I've learnt to do over the years ... is to actually physically remove myself because she will keep coming at me, or trying to meet her needs.*

Similarly, Wally disclosed a need to physically withdraw:

> *Back out, leave the room ... It just allows me to not become so emotionally overwhelmed.*

A Distinctive Dynamic

Murray revealed that he often became defensive when he felt that he was being 'accused of doing something wrong':

It's very easy to get defensive ... if it goes from a discussion to more an accusation of what you're doing wrong, then that's where I probably don't want to talk about it.

The majority of NT participants described that they dealt with their partner/family members unresponsive and avoidant behaviours through learning to become very direct, giving explicit instructions and increasing their prompting practices. Mia shared her knowledge regarding the autism spectrum, revealing that learning to prompt in very direct ways helped to prevent her partner's self-protective behaviours:

The way I talk about my needs and the way that I request some responses from him is very direct ... Previously, I wasn't ... That was before he had the diagnosis and we had the knowledge of the way he thinks and functions and our differences.

Georgia, on the other hand, shared that she overcame unresponsive behaviour by being patient and increasing her prompting behaviours:

When I ask him something, don't expect an answer straight away, just give him the time to process and sometimes you have to actually prod and give him clues.

Chapter Synopsis

This chapter focused on the second theme 'prompting triggers', examining what leads to the strategies of prompting with prompt dependency or prompt avoidance and why these strategies become the main way people communicate with each other in these relationships. Also explored were the consequences of using these strategies. The next chapter builds on this theme by showing what situations maintain the behaviours of prompting and prompt dependency and/or prompt avoidance, how participants cope with being stuck in the resulting communication difficulties, and what happens to each based on the coping strategies they choose.

7

Self-Protective Triggers

'You are completely at choice who you will
be today in your interactions with others.
Compassionate, kind, giving and forgiving will
create one set of probabilities; angry, judgemental,
critical and defensive will create another one
altogether.'
Marianne Williamson

Have The Numbers Gone Nuts?

Miscommunication is something we all deal with, but for autistic people, it can be much more complex. A study by Robertson et al. (2018) showed how miscommunication can significantly increase anxiety for many people with autism. However, this anxiety increasing miscommunication is often multifaceted. While autistic individuals may find it difficult to express their thoughts and feelings in a way that others easily understand, they can also struggle to interpret what others are trying to say, especially when the message isn't clear. This back-and-forth struggle with communication often fuels anxiety, furthering the fear of mistakes.

For autistic people, expressing themselves in a way that non-autistic people can quickly grasp is often a challenge. Since it is well known that conversations can move too quickly for them, this can leave them struggling to keep up. Non-verbal cues, sarcasm or implied meanings might not come across the way they are intended. These complications can lead to frustration, a sense of failure and even more anxiety. Additionally, since many autistic individuals also find it hard to read the emotions or intentions of others, the subtle hints or cues that non-autistic people naturally pick up on may go unnoticed. This can cause misunderstandings on both sides and, again, increase anxiety. When miscommunication happens, it can create a vicious cycle. Autistic individuals may start to feel anxious about the possibility of misunderstandings or conflicts, and this anxiety can actually make it even harder to communicate. This ever-increasing cycle can affect not just their day-to-day lives but also their relationships.

Self-Protective Triggers

Talking Tensions

The survey and interview data supported earlier studies showing that adults with ASC often face more intense communication challenges in their close relationships. These challenges can add to the stress and anxiety associated with the expectations of having to participate in personal or emotional conversations (Attwood, 2015; Lamport & Zlomke, 2014; Robertson et al., 2018). Many autistic participants seem to cope by either avoiding communication or relying heavily on prompts from their NT partner or family members, while at other times using self-protective behaviours. The analysis pointed to social anxiety as one of the main reasons behind these patterns.

Survey responses in Chapter 3 (SI 6; Figure 3.1 and SI 52; Figure 3.2) show that people with ASC usually feel more anxious than NT people during conversations. However, Figures 7.1 to 7.3 reveal that both ASC and NT individuals experience similar levels of stress when trying to talk with each other, especially about their relationship issues. Survey items 45, 49 and 50 highlight that both groups often feel intimidated, stressed and powerless when interacting with each other. A total of 60% ASC respondents and 70% NT respondents said communication with each other caused stress (Figure 7.1). Also, 68% of ASC and 59% of NT respondents felt intimidated (Figure 7.2), while 55% of ASC and 66% of NT respondents felt powerless when trying to discuss relationship difficulties (Figure 7.3).

Have The Numbers Gone Nuts?

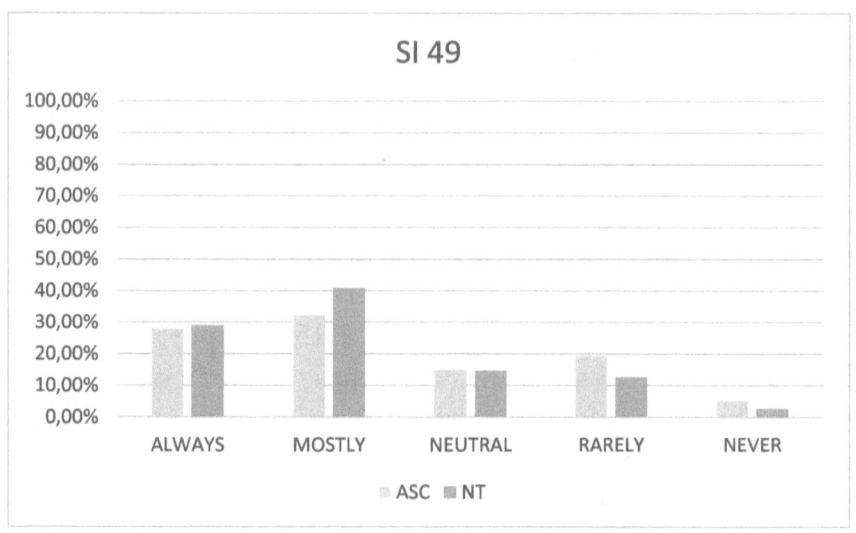

Figure 7.1. SI 49. My attempts to communicate with my partner/family member triggers stress for me.

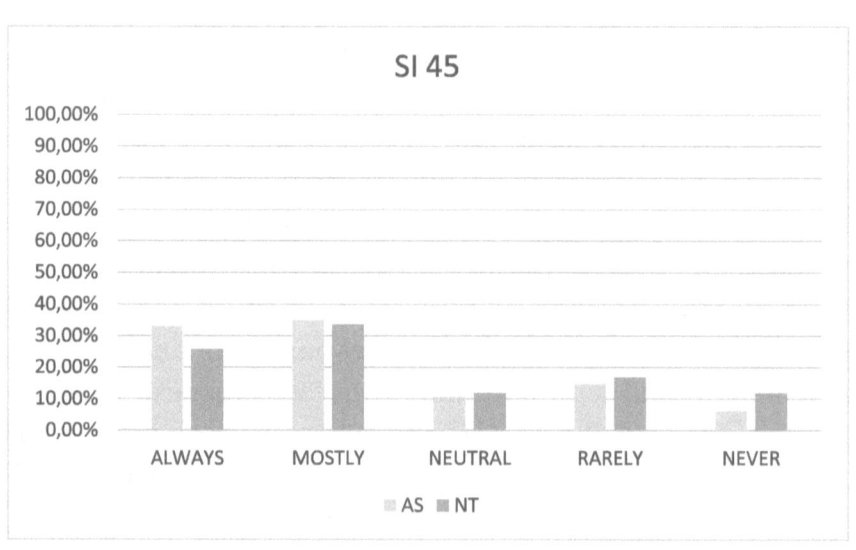

Figure 7.2. SI 45. I feel intimidated when I attempt to speak about difficulties between us.

Self-Protective Triggers

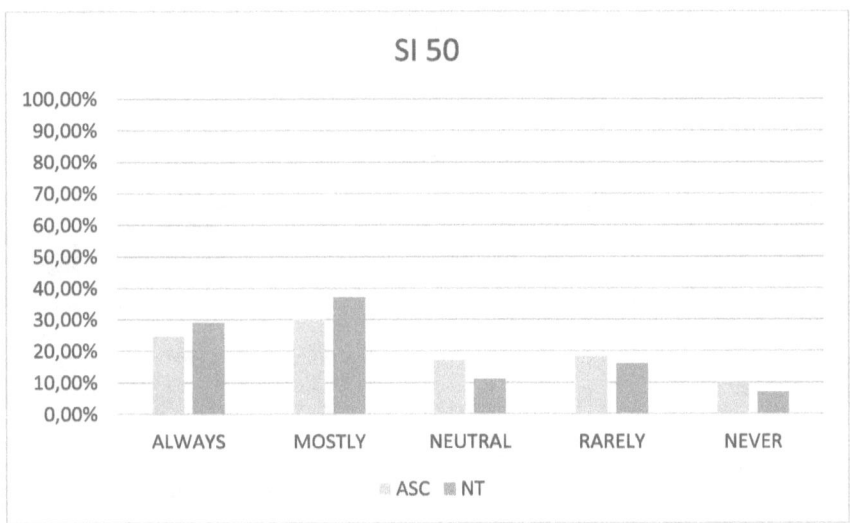

Figure 7.3. SI 50. I feel powerless to speak to my partner/ family member about the difficulties between us.

Tables 7.1, 7.2 and 7.3 illustrate gender did not appear to greatly affect the feelings of being stressed, intimidated and powerless when talking with each other. The results in these tables show that, whether male or female, most people in neurodiverse relationships felt the same way when attempting to talk with each other.

Have The Numbers Gone Nuts?

	ASC Female	%	ASC Male	%	NT Female	%	NT Male	%
Always	19	36	6	16	69	30	2	14
Mostly	12	23	17	45	92	40	8	57
Neutral	7	13	7	18	34	15	2	14
Rarely	10	19	8	21	29	13	2	14
Never	5	9	0	0	7	3	0	0
Total	53		38		231		14	

Table 7.1. My attempts to communicate with my partner/family member triggers stress for me.

	ASC Female	%	ASC Male	%	NT Female	%	NT Male	%
Always	19	35	12	32	58	25	5	36
Mostly	19	35	13	34	78	34	4	29
Neutral	3	6	6	16	29	13	0	0
Rarely	9	17	5	13	38	17	3	21
Never	4	7	2	5	27	12	2	14
Total	54		38		230		14	

Table 7.2. I feel intimidated when I attempt to speak about difficulties between us.

Self-Protective Triggers

	ASC Female	%	ASC Male	%	NT Female	%	NT Male	%
Always	13	25	9	24	69	30	2	14
Mostly	15	28	13	34	87	38	4	29
Neutral	7	13	9	24	24	10	3	21
Rarely	10	19	6	16	36	16	3	21
Never	8	15	1	3	15	6	2	14
Total	53		38		231		14	

Table 7.3. I feel powerless to speak to my partner/family member about the difficulties between us.

Talking More or Less

Although it is well known that many people with ASC feel anxious during conversations and fear making mistakes (Attwood, 2015; Lamport & Zlomke, 2014), the survey and interviews showed that this fear often led to conversation avoidance in their relationships. Interviews with ASC participants confirmed that they withdraw from conversations to keep a sense of control over their fears. Both ASC and NT participants reported similar feelings during their conversations with each other, but for different reasons. For ASC participants, the fear of emotional conversation, communication difficulties and stress from misunderstandings were the main reasons behind their feelings of anxiety and powerlessness. On the other hand, NT participants felt stressed because they had to keep prompting for interaction, often facing resistance and protective behaviours from their ASC partners and family members. Many ASC participants talked openly about their worries when it came to having conversations. Wally divulged that his fear of getting it wrong overshadowed his desire to try:

> *I don't know how to ... initiate ... it's partly probably the fear that if I ask for it and it's not given or that I'm asking and it's the wrong time and I'm talking about verbal or physical or whatever ... if I've misread that it's an inappropriate time and it's brushed off then I won't know whether it's for now or forever so...*

Rachelle described how her anxieties diminished her desire to talk with others:

> *Talking to others definitely brings on a level of anxiety and stress and it's just incredibly uncomfortable. I only want to talk to people when I need something out of them.*

Mareena disclosed how her anxieties dominated her actions:

> *With great anxiety, I'm treading on eggshells because it seems that anything I say is going to be taken the wrong way and used as a basis for further judgement.*

Most NT participants expressed frustration about always having to lead and guide conversations to make them more meaningful and personal. Many were unhappy that they had to keep prompting over time, with no real improvement. They mentioned how difficult it was to start or keep conversations going, and this constant effort left them feeling frustrated and dissatisfied. Since they had no other option but to prompt for engagement, it often led to even more prompting. Ruth lamented the necessity of prompting with instructions in order to get what she needed:

Self-Protective Triggers

I wish I didn't have to prompt him ... but I realise that is the reality of my life ... He needs instructions, so if I provide them, he can usually follow them in his own way ... It would be great if he could say these things without prompting, but I know that may never happen.

Ronda also protested the need to prompt her husband into having conversations with her, and that he remained dependent on her prompts in all aspects:

The initiation for entering into any kind of communication was always me. Conversation starter is always me, and initiation for calling or Skyping will always be me and he just waits until I call ... I've tested that over the years to see if I stop, will he start, and the answer is – no he will not. So, if I don't initiate then there is nothing, and that's in all aspects of our marriage.

Hit and Miss

When prompting worked sometimes but not others, it usually led NT participants to prompt even more over time. Since occasional success tends to make people try harder, prompting became the main way NT participants kept conversations going in their relationships. In contrast, when asked if they ever felt the need to prompt conversations or make connections, most ASC participants gave brief 'no' answers. However, a few shared some reasons why they might occasionally use prompting in their conversations:

SAMUEL *Yeah, few and far between. I don't generally prompt conversation apart from the necessary small talk to get on together.*

Have The Numbers Gone Nuts?

> TERRY *The only time I've needed to prompt her is if she is in a bad mood and I'm trying to make up because it's quite likely she's in a bad mood because of something I've done or said, or not done or not said.*

When NT participants were asked within the interviews if their ASC partner/family members had prompted conversations, similar to ASC participants, most said no.

> DAWN *No not really. No that's one thing that I noticed, that I will say 'You are really frustrating me because …' or 'I am really unhappy because …' and he never, ever says anything like that. He never brings it up.*

A few, however, described the occasional circumstance when their partner/family members with ASC had done so, and their perception of motivations for doing so:

> SOPHIE *I think most of the time that he prompts conversation is when the response or decision is directly affecting him. For example, the ever so common, 'What do you want to do for dinner', conversation.*

Self-Protective Triggers

Chapter Synopsis

This chapter continued exploring the second theme 'prompting triggers', which investigated the conditions that cause prompting and prompt dependency and/or prompt avoidance to become the main communication strategy within these relationships. The next chapter looks at the third theme: 'a prompt dependency cycle'. It explores what circumstances activate these strategies to form into a communication cycle, what tactics participants use to deal with being entangled in the cycle and what transpires as a result of the choice of tactics used.

8

Competitive Loops

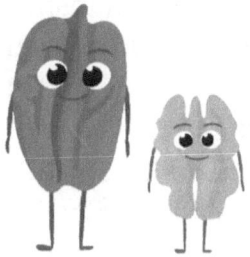

'You cannot protect yourself from sadness without
protecting yourself from happiness.'
Jonathan Safran Foer

Have The Numbers Gone Nuts?

According to Jaswal and Akhtar (2019), it is questionable to assume that autistic people are all socially unmotivated. Although many autistic people do not seem as interested in social interactions as non-autistic people do, this assumption does not match what some autistic people say about their own experiences. As Wally (ASC) said:

Don't get the idea that all people with autism just want to sit and rock in the corner. We quite like to be social but we're really shit at it.

Research also suggests that autistic people may experience rewards differently, which could affect their social connections, and they may have fewer close friendships. However, the idea that these behaviours are driven by less social motivation or interest has some flaws as social motivation is not just about the individual, it is shaped by how the person interacts with and is perceived by others, making it a more complex, dynamic process than simply an internal trait.

That said, the social interaction needs of those with ASC can differ significantly from the NT population (Mendes, 2015). In these studies, these different needs were found to create an incompatible relational dynamic. The needs of one to have a large amount of emotional interaction and build warmth and connection within their relationship was diametrically opposed to the needs of the other to have a large amount of solitude and silence. Additionally, a need to address issues was also diametrically opposed to a need to avoid issues. The result of this pairing of incompatible needs within a relationship was a power struggle as each tried to get their opposing needs met, which in turn, triggered a multitude of unresolvable differences and subsequent compensatory strategies.

Competitive Loops

The survey and interview results supported earlier research (Canevello & Crocker, 2010; Mendes, 2015), showing that when there is a lack of responsiveness in relationships it can create serious tension. In neurodiverse relationships this tension was intensified by a tug-of-war between wanting connection and wanting to avoid it at the same time. This back-and-forth dynamic seems to be a core factor in creating the opposing forces between prompting and prompt dependency or prompt avoidance, where interactions between ASC and NT people do not align.

In these situations, NT people tend to keep prompting, while autistic people tend to either avoid these prompts or become dependent on them. The result is an ongoing pattern where NT people feel they need to encourage conversation or action, and autistic people can feel stressed or anxious about it, leading to complex, circular interactions. There is often a power struggle, where one person wants things to stay the same, while the other wants change. This clash fuels the prompt dependency cycle, creating a challenging communication pattern within these relationships.

A Pervasive Tug-of-War

The interview and survey results confirmed past research (Domingue & Mollen, 2009; Egan & Linenberg, 2019; Gillberg et al., 2015), showing that the unresponsive or avoidant behaviours that autistic individuals often employ can become deeply ingrained. Neurotypical participants described trying to overcome these behaviours by intensifying their efforts to prompt interaction through using supportive coaching to encourage connection and offer help when needed.

Have The Numbers Gone Nuts?

However, instead of encouraging more engagement, these increased efforts often led those with ASC to either become dependent on prompting, and therefore only engage when prompted, or else become even more withdrawn, unresponsive or self-protective. In some cases, NT participants said they accepted defeat and started avoiding interaction themselves. Other times, the occasional success of prompting created a cycle, where autistic individuals would either depend on the prompts or avoid them, maintaining this back-and-forth dynamic. Sometimes those with ASC showed a growing pattern of behaviours like avoiding conversations, getting defensive, shutting down or even becoming verbally aggressive. These responses seemed to spark a series of reactions, including some actions that felt 'out of character' (Figures 6.1, 6.6, 6.8, 6.9 and 6.10, in Chapter 6). About 57% of ASC respondents and 29% of NT respondents reported acting this way (Figure 8.1). Interviews indicated that these connected behaviours created a communication cycle, leading to the development of various coping strategies. These strategies helped people in neurodiverse relationships manage the ongoing and often building challenges they faced.

Competitive Loops

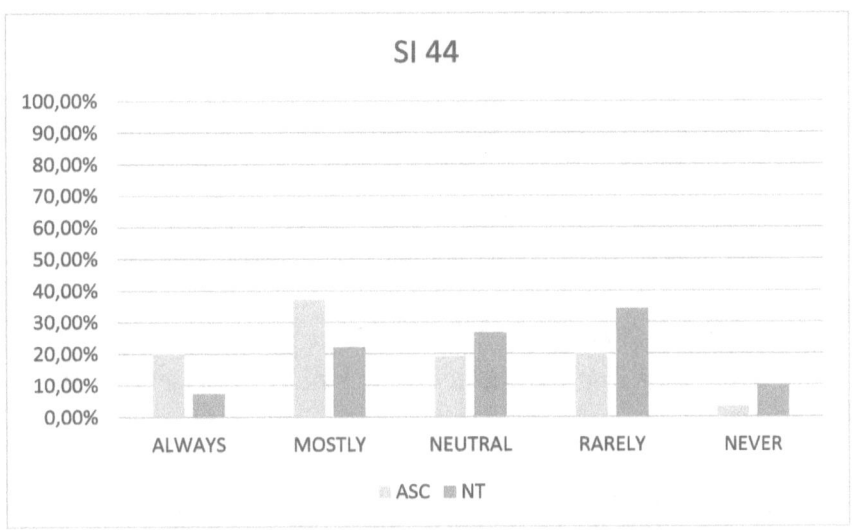

Figure 8.1. SI 44. I behave out of character when having difficult conversations.

Detachment Dangers

Several ASC participants talked about their habit of withdrawing from communication, but many did not seem to realise how these 'stonewalling' actions could harm their relationships. They also seemed unaware that their partner or family members were trying to connect with them, which further blocked meaningful connection. This lack of awareness not only made it harder for their partners and family members to feel satisfied in the relationship, but it also led to feelings of dissatisfaction for the ASC participants themselves, who often felt they weren't getting the alone time they needed. For instance, Samuel shared that his diagnosis led him to become even 'more stand-offish'.

Have The Numbers Gone Nuts?

> *After the diagnosis I became more stand-offish ... in knowing that I'm wired differently and in order to act normally is a real strain. I'd rather just save my energy and enjoy myself doing what I want.*

Terry divulged how he avoided interaction by 'zoning out':

> *Well, I tend to back off and sort of zone out at times ... I'm noticing that I do tend to withdraw a lot, in those sorts of situations.*

Tom disclosed that difficult conversations can incentivise him to use stonewalling tactics:

> *Sometimes difficult conversations cause me to feel attacked and I respond defensively and sometimes angrily ... I tell him I don't want to talk about it anymore.*

However, Matt shared a different perspective:

> *You know if you don't have the humility to respond to your external suggestions you don't improve ... If you're not prepared to be humble to some extent then whether you're on the spectrum or whether you're neurotypical the lack of humility will inevitably affect the relationship ... but I think to some extent you also have to go to a place where you're not comfortable.*

Many of these stonewalling actions were described by NT participants. Maggie drew attention to the different stonewalling approaches that her partner used, as opposed to her daughter:

Competitive Loops

Whenever I want to talk about anything that's emotional, he will either shut down or just change the subject ... My daughter tends to get angry, more than my husband ... she's also more aggressive ... Luke will sit there and pretend and try, whereas ... she tends to ... just shut me out.

Whereas Debra's account of her ex-partner and her son, revealed variations in a different way:

[My ex-partner] seems to be really needy about me, and always has been ... If I call him or if I send him a note, he responds immediately ... He can't wait to talk to me. [My son] is a little bit less inclined to do that ... He likes to be really demonstrative about not responding.

Surviving the Discord

Emotional conversation avoidance, while it may help people with ASC feel safer, was found to regularly go hand in hand with other behaviours. For example, an avoidance of asking personal questions, could lead to inaccurate assumptions about others. In turn, these behaviours can form into a pattern of conversation avoidance that seems to become the main way of coping in the cycle of prompt dependency. In response, NT participants reported putting a lot of effort into planning and preparing conversations, along with managing the relationship dynamics in ways that go far beyond typical interactions. This careful planning eventually became the main strategy they used to cope within the prompt dependency cycle.

Have The Numbers Gone Nuts?

The Demise of Personal Questions

For those with ASC, avoidance techniques such as an absence of asking questions, especially personal questions, often led to misinterpreting others' actions, and making inaccurate assumptions. Although it was understood that these avoidance behaviours were intended to help manage social challenges by preventing emotional conversations, instead they appeared to have the opposite effect. Since NT participants were attempting to increase emotional conversations, prompting continued to increase and the avoidance techniques ASC participants used only served to further complicate most interactions.

According to survey data, 58% of ASC respondents said they always or mostly seek clarification by asking questions (SI 8; Figure 8.2). However, this survey finding does not fully match the interview feedback. Most ASC and NT participants in interviews noted that a common issue for ASC participants was not asking personal questions. This difference between survey and interview results also was observed when it came to the value placed on deep, meaningful conversations by each group (SI 34; Figure 2.5 in Chapter 2). It may reflect a pattern where those with ASC may understand the importance of certain social behaviours but do not always put them into practice, possibly because of different social needs and abilities compared to NT individuals.

For ASC individuals, asking questions to share information is often a strong point, but asking questions related to relationships seems to be a limitation. On the other hand, 95% of NT respondents reported they always or mostly seek clarification by asking questions, which aligns closely with NT interview responses. For the NT population, asking questions can be a way to connect deeply with others by gaining insight into their inner world, an area where they typically excel. In addition, asking questions also serves as a form of prompting in conversation.

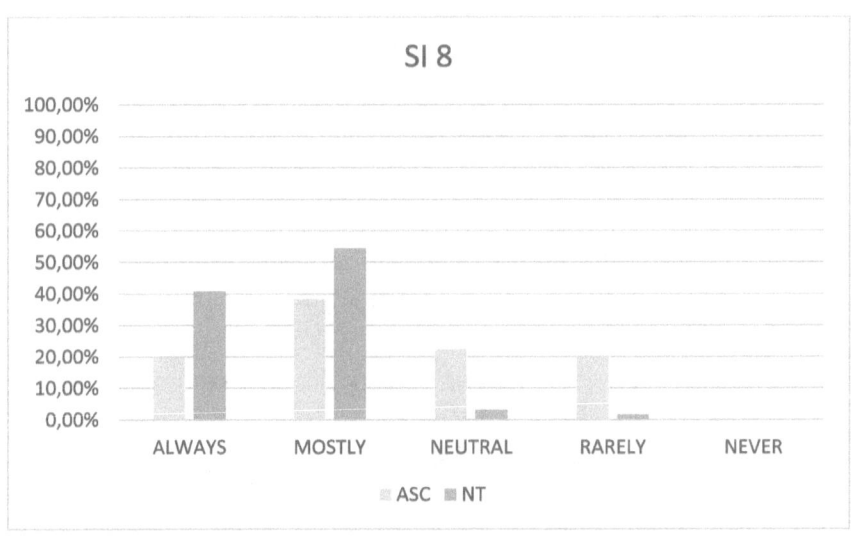

Figure 8.2. SI 8. When someone says something that I'm not sure about, I ask for clarification.

ASC participants shared that they used stonewalling behaviours such as shutting down or withdrawing, as a way to protect themselves. Instead of asking questions, stonewalling allowed them to avoid difficult or unwanted conversations entirely. However, they often did not realise that this protective behaviour actually trapped them deeper into the cycle of prompt dependency, where avoiding questions or prompts from their partner or family only reinforced the cycle.

Ironically, both ASC and NT participants reported that avoiding these interactions made the situation worse. Since

Have The Numbers Gone Nuts?

NT participants needed answers to their questions and the emotional connection they were missing, avoidance of these aspects essentially resulted in exactly what ASC people wanted to avoid. Richard (ASC) admitted he could sense when 'something was wrong', but he chose to ignore it and avoid asking questions as a way to protect himself. He did not appear to fully realise that by avoiding his partner's questions, he was actually making it more likely that she would keep 'pushing' and asking or prompting.

> *But if I can sort of see something is wrong, I don't ask questions ... She requires an answer ... pushing and pushing ... It gets too annoying, sometimes an argument.*

Terry showed insight that asking questions and asking for clarification would help him understand better; still he revealed that he did not often recognise when to ask for clarification:

> *Kim would like me to take the lead with conversation at times and ask questions rather than hang back ... If she says something that I take literally ... [I] don't ... recognise, I don't understand and I need more information, and to actually stop and ask for clarification.*

The interconnected life that NT participants longed to share with their partner/family members was a frequent casualty of the lack of interpersonal questions. However, their need to be emotionally connected with their partner and family members meant that prompting was unavoidable. Sabrina shared, that even though her endeavours were frequently unsuccessful, prompting with questions was her preferred option to the 'staring quiet' otherwise conveyed:

Competitive Loops

No matter how many different ways I try to ask him 'well what would you...?' I read one of the books and I tried one of the techniques about asking them how they would feel and it doesn't help, it gives me more of... which I hate, that uncomfortable staring quiet.

Similarly, while Mandy observed that her questions caused her to be 'in trouble', she also noted that her partner did not ask her about her concerns:

He won't come to me and say 'You're cranky. What's wrong?' ... I'm always in trouble for asking too many questions but if I don't ask, I don't know anything.

Mix-Ups and Slip-Ups

The survey and interview findings confirmed what previous research (Attwood, 2015; Zamzow et al., 2016), has shown: the challenges people with ASC face in social interactions, such as difficulties with reciprocity and a need to disengage from conversations, often led to misunderstandings in relationships. These difficulties can make it easier to misinterpret others' actions and form inaccurate assumptions based on those misunderstandings. The study pointed to a few contributing factors: not asking questions (Figure 8.3), expecting conversations to be more literal than intended (Figure 8.4), getting stuck in unproductive conversations (SI 23; Figure 5.4 in Chapter 5), avoiding certain discussions (SI 38; Figure 6.1 in Chapter 6), reacting unexpectedly (SI 46; Figure 6.4 in Chapter 6) and dismissing explanations (SI 54; Figure 6.5 in Chapter 6). Together, these tendencies seem to play a significant role in creating misunderstandings.

Have The Numbers Gone Nuts?

When asked about waiting for information versus asking questions, 43% of ASC and 39% of NT respondents thought waiting was more productive (Figure 8.3). Meanwhile, 63% of ASC respondents and 65% of NT respondents agreed that both sides shared equal responsibility when communication issues arose (Figure 8.4). Although each of these factors alone might not always cause misunderstandings or wrong assumptions, combined with behaviours such as avoiding certain topics, reacting unexpectedly, disregarding explanations and unresolved discussions (Figures 5.4 in Chapter 5; 6.1, 6.4 and 6.5 in Chapter 6), they can create many opportunities to misinterpret situations.

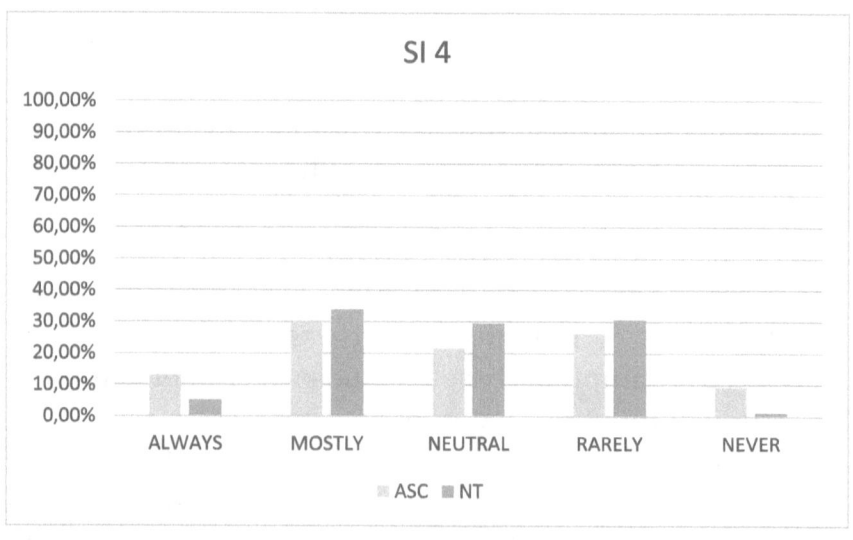

Figure 8.3. SI 4. If unsure of what someone is saying to me, rather than ask questions, I will wait to learn more.

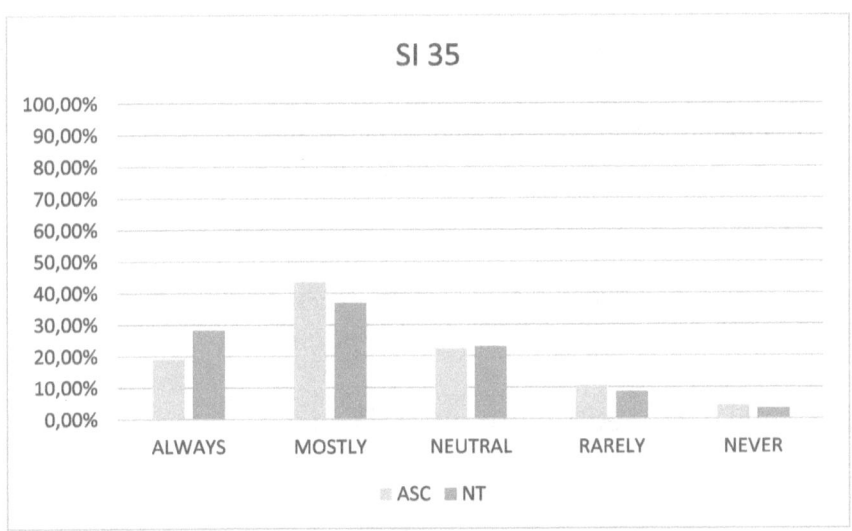

Figure 8.4. SI 35. Although I use precise and accurate statements, I am held responsible for communication difficulties.

Interviews suggested that people with ASC often did not realise they had made assumptions or did not know how to clear up misunderstandings that came from their assumptions. They also were not aware that taking time to ask questions in conversations could help avoid these misunderstandings. Learning to ask information-gathering questions could make it so their partner or family member would not need to prompt them as much, breaking the habit of relying on prompts.

Sharon assumed that confusion was caused when discussing her problems with others:

> *I don't like to burden other people with my problems ... it confused them when I start to talk to them about my*

problems. I am also usually the most rational person among people I know, and their highly emotional reaction toward my problem can be very ineffective for me.

Barry assumed that a difference of opinion signified stupidity:

Because it's almost like if someone doesn't see the thing the way that I do, I just think they are stupid.

Rachelle assumed that others talk just to 'hear their own voices':

I just try and withdraw from conversation at work because people tend to talk about the same things over and over again … it's so shallow and minor as well. They're just talking to hear their own voices sometimes.

Many NT participants shared that they felt the lack of questions was the main reason for many of the misunderstandings that happened, which often led to conversations, actions and events being misinterpreted. Most said that having to constantly prompt or guide conversations to sort out these assumptions often caused conflicts. Dawn talked about how her partner's tendency to assume things based on his misreading of events impacted her day-to-day life:

He takes away what can be a completely different perception of what I have said and … he doesn't ask me anything, my feelings or thoughts on things and then makes sweeping assumptions. I mean I have heard him telling somebody 'Oh, Dawn thinks blah, blah, blah' and I am like 'I never said that. Where did that come from?'… That's not uncommon and he has … obviously heard my voice in his head saying

Competitive Loops

'Dawn likes A' instead of asking Dawn if she likes A or B and finding out that she likes B and so he makes these sweeping assumptions ... about me without checking on them first.

Maggie disclosed the strategies that she implemented in order to cope with the aftermaths of incorrect assumptions, both from her daughter and her husband:

My husband has conversations with me in his head and then vows and declares that that's what I've said and I used to think I was going crazy because I don't remember these conversations until I worked it out ... but for [my daughter] ... I have to have things written down which is why I like the text ... if she says one thing and then she says another I can turn round and say, 'No you said this, see, check the text message that you said it', and she'll check it and go 'Oh!'

Ronda made an interesting point about how misinterpretations can occur:

Some researchers ... said [that] a major source of their social misunderstandings is because they jump to conclusions too quickly and they jump to the wrong conclusion.

Guided Conversations

To deal with their partner or family member's lack of participation in conversations, and the misunderstandings that followed, NT participants described how they invested a significant amount of effort in trying to overturn misinterpretations and to keep communication going. This meant that they spent time carefully planning conversations, adding prompts and ways to keep the relationship stable, which they found were the main ways they managed these challenges. Since family members or partners with ASC often resisted deeper conversations, all NT interviewees shared that they felt they had to 'prepare' before most important discussions, especially those that were emotional or involved significant decisions. This preparation became their primary approach, helping them deal with self-protective or dependent behaviours while attempting to influence some semblance of relating. Winnie shared her strategy in giving repeated reminders:

> *If the issues come up ... that we need to discuss as a couple, then I will assess the time when it is a 'good time' to set aside time to talk about that and I will warn him about that so that he can prepare ... I will just mention for a few days in advance, you know we need to talk about this ... we have better conversations and he will sit and participate in a conversation if I do that preparatory work.*

Likewise, Haley shared her recipe for success:

> *I had to censor everything before I actually attempted to tell him something and I had to make sure I worded it so that it didn't come across like I was attacking ... I'd either write down some dot points and I made sure that I stuck to them or I would just make sure in my head I had it straight exactly what I need to say to him you know and I always started with, 'I don't want you to react, I want you to listen to what I have got to say. I don't want your opinion either. I just need you to listen and then process it and then I will ask you to make a choice.'*

Georgia reported that her conversation preparation involved becoming proficient at 'conversational scene setting', being

Competitive Loops

cautious with the words that she used and intercepting conversations that go off track:

> *I have to precede ... 'I'm not criticising', and learning how to say your sentences in a way that's not threatening to them, and then if you were to get it wrong then the shit hits the fan, because you've said it in the wrong way, or with the wrong tone of voice, and they feel threatened, or they feel you're criticising them or you're undermining, and it's like, 'Oh my God! You're worse than a teenager.'*

Lilly explained that slowing her discussions down worked for her:

> *I try to slow my voice down. I try to give one instruction at a time. I try to wait for his responses. Sometimes you know I mess up and start going on the next thing too.*

Chapter Synopsis

This chapter explored theme three, 'a prompt dependency cycle' which examined what sets the communication cycle in motion. It showed how giving prompts, avoiding them, or relying on them can lead to a back-and-forth communication pattern. These opposing behaviours, where each person tries to meet their own needs through the giving of prompts in combination with avoiding them or relying on them, are what drive the cycle. The next chapter builds on this theme by looking at some of the effects of being stuck in this kind of communication system.

9

Disastrous Developments

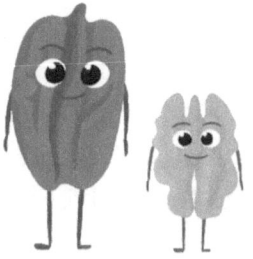

'No relationship in this world ever remains warm and close unless good effort is made on both sides to keep it so.'
Eleanor Roosevelt

Have The Numbers Gone Nuts?

The main effect of each group's converging coping strategies was a cycle of prompt dependency. In this cycle, most conversations became trapped in an oppositional dynamic, with each person trying to meet their own different and opposing needs. For the ASC participants, this led to constantly fluctuating between complying with prompts, avoiding them, or trying to avoid any conflict that might arise. Meanwhile, the NT participants found themselves putting in a lot more communicational effort, usually beyond what is customary within close relationships. Over time, this back-and-forth communication system created a cyclic pattern which resulted in the NT participants needing to take on a parental or caretaker role.

At Cross Purposes

A majority of both ASC (57%) and NT (79%) respondents felt that they often found themselves in circular conversations that did not reach any real conclusion (Figure 9.1). Most NT participants tried to cope with these situations by steering or guiding the conversation, as shown in Figures 6.2 and 6.3 in Chapter 6. The interviews revealed that NT participants frequently felt the need to guide conversations because many ASC family members or partners tended to avoid certain topics. However, this approach sometimes backfired and actually led to more circular conversations, as prompting and guiding didn't always get the results NT participants were hoping for.

Disastrous Developments

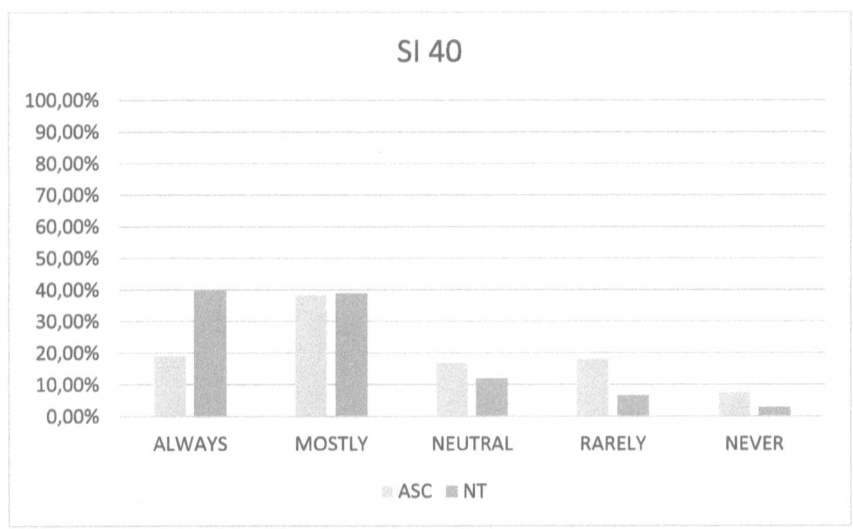

Figure 9.1. SI 40. Conversations tend to go around and around without coming to a satisfactory conclusion.

While it was a topic that not many ASC participants discussed, a few shared some valuable insights into their perspective on the un-resolvability of their cyclic disagreements. When asked about circular conversations, Stella described how constant and unresolvable their circular conversations were:

> *We raise the same topics over and over again – child rearing, money and chores and it seems that we never reach a final conclusion.*

Terry outlined the escalating nature of some of his cyclic types of conversations:

> *I have one point of view and she has another one. Whether it's one person is right or wrong or whether it's a communication misunderstanding again we get this sort of 'ratcheting up' scenario that seems to happen.*

Have The Numbers Gone Nuts?

In contrast, the majority of NT participants had a lot to say on the topic. Haley described how the progress of time had only made the circumstances worse:

> *[We] couldn't get off the merry-go-round and ended up ... in a screaming match ... I used to try and reason, like as a normal person would ... In the end ... it had to stop because it was just going on and on in circles.*

Likewise, Ronda recalled how their 'ridiculous crazy circles' did not achieve a resolution:

> *There was never any resolution, they just went around in circles because he was never addressing the actual topic ... probably didn't understand where I was trying to go ... Just going around in these ridiculous crazy circles all evening.*

Shirley also described 'endless cycles' of miscommunication:

> *So many of our arguments ... are based on misunderstandings and we just keep getting into a cycle of 'but I didn't mean that, I meant this', 'well that's not how I took it, I felt this' and it just keeps going around and around ... we get stuck in these endless cycles of the same kind of arguments.*

Sabrina expressed it as a 'dog chasing its tail' that they cannot escape:

> *We just end up in this, it's the dog chasing its tail ... when it's about us and our relationship it's just a circle that we can't get out of.*

Disastrous Developments

An Arising Burden

The extra effort that NT participants had to invest into communication in their relationships often lead to an uneven dynamic. Responses to SI 21 show that while autistic people generally do not feel like they take on a caregiver role in their relationships, most NT people do (Figure 9.2). A total of 49% of autistic respondents said they rarely or never felt like a relational caretaker, whereas 91% of NT respondents said they always or mostly felt that way.

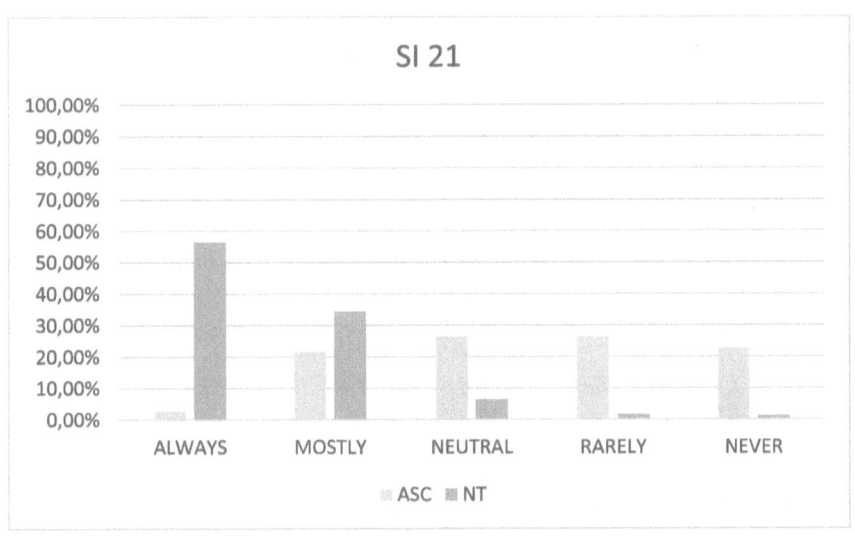

Figure 9.2. SI 21. I feel that I am the relationship caretaker and manager.

Although more NT and ASC women than men said they felt like they were a relational caretaker, the majority of autistic men and women did not feel that they took on a caretaker role in their relationships. However, most NT men and women did feel this way (Table 9.1).

Have The Numbers Gone Nuts?

	ASC Female	%	ASC Male	%	NT Female	%	NT Male	%
Always	3	5	0	0	137	58	4	29
Mostly	17	26	6	15	81	34	5	36
Neutral	22	34	6	15	13	6	3	21
Rarely	13	20	13	33	2	.85	2	14
Never	10	15	14	36	3	1	0	0
Total	65		39		236		14	

Table 9.1. I feel that I am the relationship caretaker and manager.

While most ASC participants did not discuss this asymmetrical feature of their relationships, Wally did have some thoughts that he shared on the matter:

> *When I get into that state, I need support from her which she may not be willing to give and she shouldn't have to ... It puts her into that caring role rather than an equal role and that's unfair. It's me imposing that need on her that she shouldn't have to deal with and it's become a real barrier. Interesting talking about this stuff because that's what it is, it's that fear of being the needy one.*

All NT participants in the study said they felt responsible for taking on a main caretaker role in their relationship, with some even comparing it to a parent-child dynamic. Lucy expressed the general NT point of view:

> *You've just got to point it out to him. He just doesn't get it because he's so focused on him. I guess that's the childlike way that they go about things ... I believe that yes, I am the*

major caretaker ... being the caretaker of the emotional side ... but I seem to be the one working at it all the time ... I don't understand, it's very childish ... unless we're talking about his stuff it's as if they're of little interest to him.

The majority of NT participants mentioned similar impressions of feeling more like a mother to their partner/family members with ASC:

SABRINA *It's like having a conversation with a child ... and I feel like I'm mothering him and I don't want to be that person but ... I'm like 'stop acting like a 15-year-old', so the conversation is like with a kid.*

QUINN *And I was telling him this week it almost feels like when I have conversations with him about our relationship, it feels like a mum and a child ... I have 3 children with him, I have 3 boys, ... he's my 4th child.*

Chapter Synopsis

This chapter has presented some of the results of being caught up in the communication system that results from the combination of prompting with prompt dependency and/or prompt avoidance behaviours. The following chapter presents theme four which describes the additional cycles that form as a result of being caught within the prompt dependency communication cycle.

10

Complicated Additions

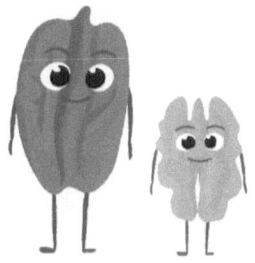

'Perhaps one did not want to be loved
so much as to be understood.'
George Orwell

Have The Numbers Gone Nuts?

Research has shown that when autistic and neurotypical people interact, they often have trouble understanding, empathising with and being understood by each other (Kimura et al., 2020; Lawson et al., 2004). It was found that due to the particular problems that resulted from failures to understand each other in neurodiverse relationships, a pattern where the person with ASC became overly reliant on prompts from the other developed, creating a cycle of dependency or avoidance that operated alongside the prompting. This cycle became a back-and-forth power struggle, where each person's needs competed for attention. As a result, most of their conversations and interactions were affected and repeated communication loops emerged.

Cycles Within Cycles

The circling communication patterns formed due to the different approaches to emotional connection. This dynamic created additional ongoing cycles of interaction that emerged alongside the prompt-dependency pattern. Essentially, these interactions revolved around either relying on or steering clear of prompts, becoming a defining feature of how they communicated. The push to maintain emotional boundaries kept this pattern going, making it a lasting part of interactions. The additional cycles that formed were found to be the 'imitating normalcy cycle', the 'stonewalling cycle', the 'help seeking cycle', and the 'loss of sense of self cycle'.

The Imitating Normalcy Cycle

Both ASC and NT participants worked to appear socially acceptable. For example, responses to SI 13 (Chapter 2, Figure 2.1), SI 9 (Chapter 4, Figure 4.9), and SI 16 (Chapter 10, Figure

Complicated Additions

10.1) highlighted known social differences between the two groups. Despite this, the interviews revealed that both groups tried to seem 'normal' in public.

Both ASC and NT participants also noted a difference between how autistic individuals behaved at work compared to at home. This gap between public and private behaviour emphasised the effort to appear normal but also deepened the sense of division within the home. This division was closely tied to the cycles of prompting and self-protection. NT participants mentioned providing support to handle social gaps for their autistic partners or family members, which further reinforced the disconnect between public and private life. Richard (ASC) explained that:

On the movie Prince Charming and Snow White ... they get together, they have the big wedding and go off into the sunset and you don't see the rest of their life together ... We get information on whether you're suitable for marriage ... but the actual ... married life ... and what's normal ... you're pretty much learning things as you go along.

Survey responses showed that less than half of the respondents with ASC (47%) said they were aware of social rules (see Figure 10.1). However, during the interviews, it became clear that many NT people took on the role of teaching these social rules to help their ASC partners or family members understand what was expected of them. The interviews also supported Richard's observation that people with ASC often don't fully grasp the social norms needed to maintain close relationships. In contrast, 98% of NT respondents indicated that they were always or mostly aware of social rules, with more than half (58%), saying they were always aware. The interviews confirmed these survey findings.

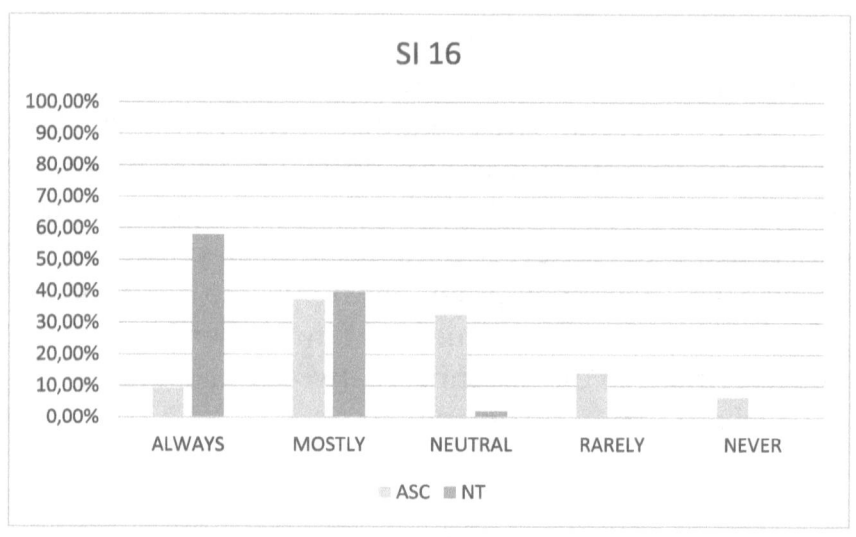

Figure 10.1. SI 16. I am aware of the rules that guide social behaviour.

Murray (ASC) explained that his NT partner had helped him to learn social rules:

> *Over time I've picked up a lot of rules ... when [my partner] has explained to me 'you shouldn't say this or you should do it that way or whatever' because I've come from being fully clueless to being I now know a lot of them intellectually ... I think for people who are on the spectrum that don't have partners that explain the rules to them they would know less of the rules ... Every social rule needs to be explained ... if my partner never explained the rules to me I literally wouldn't know them.*

Complicated Additions

Richard (ASC) and Wally (ASC) discussed differences between their public and private lives:

> RICHARD *When you go out the front door ... you put on a happy face and you say 'good day' to everybody but ... at home it could be World War 3 ... but you don't take that outside.*

> WALLY *I function well at work ... Work is the place where you know your place, you know your structure, you know your boundaries. There are limitations to the subjects that are discussed ... In your workplace you're there because you know your shit in that area, but in a family all rules are off.*

While those with ASC can benefit from the support given to them by their partner and family members in order to construct normalcy in their lives, it was a different story for NT participants. They reported that the difference between the public persona, and the person that they experienced behind closed doors, created a disconnection between the actual and feigned aspects of their lives:

> GEORGIA *You shouldn't have to tell a 54-year-old man of 3 children ... how to live his personal life in his family, a man who is capable of running a department, being the head of people, is obviously incredibly bright, manages multi-million-dollar grants, but at home is basically a child ... Work ... is their interest. They are functioning, they take initiative, they get stuff done, but when they come home, they*

> *can't do anything ... you end up being their mother.*

TRACY   *At first, I did not dare to tell anyone ... then, after seeking professional help, I felt more at ease about sharing with more people ... because James is a totally different person in public.*

The Stonewalling Cycle

Stonewalling is a tactic people use to shut down conversations and avoid further discussion. This can include ignoring the conversation, getting defensive, going silent or even becoming verbally aggressive to stop the exchange altogether. As presented in Chapter 6, autistic participants were much more likely to use these avoidant and stonewalling behaviours, while NT participants showed these behaviours far less frequently (Figures 6.1, 6.8, 6.9 and 6.10). This unresponsive behaviour was a major reason why NT participants felt the need to prompt or push their autistic partners or family members to engage, often trying to break through the avoidance and stonewalling.

The interview results confirmed what the surveys showed: most autistic and NT participants noted that autistic individuals often tried to avoid difficult or uncomfortable conversations. However, when stonewalling became more intense, it frequently led to relationship issues. Interestingly, many autistic participants didn't seem particularly concerned about these behaviours or their impact:

SANDRA   *I start to walk out of the room or I just turn over in bed and want to go to sleep ... He's*

Complicated Additions

> *told me it really bothers him ... I just want to go do something else and end that situation.*

RACHELLE *I don't want the conversation to occur ... Sometimes I tell him I don't understand why it is so much of a big issue ... He does [explain] but I still don't really get it.*

TERRY *I tend to withdraw ... it works for me but it doesn't work for Kim.*

While most NT participants said that they understood that avoidance of their conversations was not always deliberate, they also disclosed that the stonewalling behaviour shown to them, and the resulting disconnection, was a huge challenge to their relationship:

RUTH *He would prefer to not talk through issues, which I find odd ... A willingness to talk through issues and listen to the other person is important in a relationship ... Him getting defensive and shutting down, freezing, not answering questions, not talking to me, stonewalling. Sometimes he even walks away from me when I'm talking. He often forgets what we talk about.*

LAURA *He either evades or gets frightened and retreats ... His tendency to get out of uncomfortable things with small lies. His obsessive secrecy, which has grown more as we've been together, so that he just blanks me on certain topics.*

Have The Numbers Gone Nuts?

The Help Seeking Cycle

Seeking help turned out to be a complicated process for many participants. Since autism is not always visible, both ASC and NT participants often struggled with disbelief or rejection when asking for support. According to survey questions SI 30 and SI 31 (Figures 10.2 and 10.3), many respondents felt doubted when they reached out for help.

For autistic participants, 41% said this issue didn't apply to them when it came to family and friends, and 55% felt it didn't apply when dealing with professionals. However, 31% reported feeling disbelieved by family and friends, while 16% experienced this with professionals.

In comparison, a larger percentage of NT participants faced disbelief: 62% from family and friends and 35% from professionals. Only 15% of NT respondents felt that this disbelief was not applicable with family and friends, and 34% felt it was not applicable with professionals. However, when asked in interviews why they had selected 'not applicable' in their survey responses, most said it was because of concerns about scepticism.

Complicated Additions

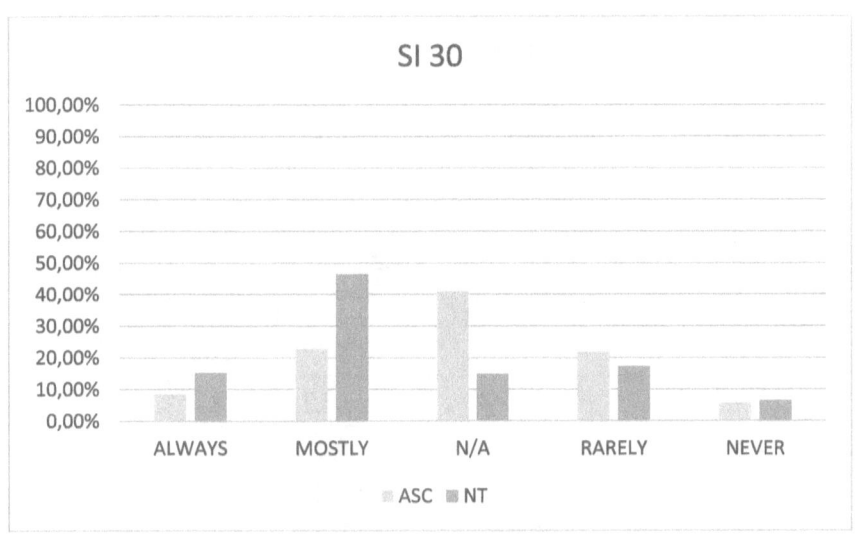

Figure 10.2. SI 30. I am not believed when describing our particular relationship difficulties to others, such as family and friends.

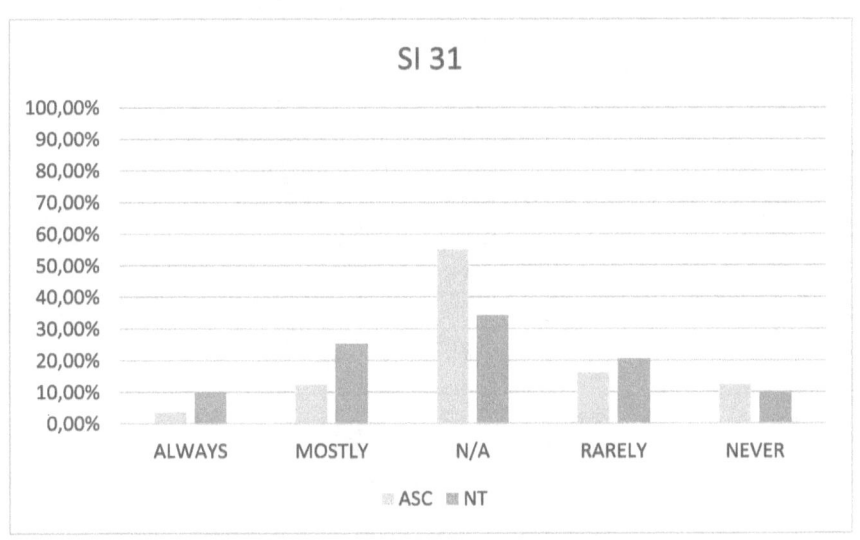

Figure 10.3. SI 31. I am not believed when seeking professional help regarding our relationship.

Have The Numbers Gone Nuts?

Although a higher percentage of ASC and NT females answered that they had experienced a lack of belief by family, friends and professionals, both males and females of both groups showed that they had experienced this lack of belief (Tables 10.1 and 10.2).

	ASC Female	%	ASC Male	%	NT Female	%	NT Male	%
Always	6	9	3	8	37	16	1	7
Mostly	17	27	7	18	112	47	4	29
Neutral	23	36	19	49	34	14	3	21
Rarely	14	22	9	23	39	17	4	29
Never	4	6	1	3	14	6	2	14
Total	64		39		236		14	

Table 10.1. I am not believed when describing our particular relationship difficulties to others, such as family and friends.

	ASC Female	%	ASC Male	%	NT Female	%	NT Male	%
Always	2	3	2	5	25	11	0	0
Mostly	10	16	3	8	62	26	1	8
Neutral	36	57	20	51	75	32	10	77
Rarely	8	12	9	23	50	21	1	8
Never	8	12	5	13	24	10	1	8
Total	64		39		236		13	

Table 10.2. I am not believed when seeking professional help regarding our relationship.

Complicated Additions

Most ASC participants stated that they did not seek help or talk to family and friends about their relationships. Those who did seek help, either through family and friends or professionally, reported varying degrees of success. When asked if he talked to friends and family about his relationship Terry said:

> *No. I've never done that; the only person I discuss my relationships with is Kim.*

However, he went on to say that he had sought professional help which was not always positive:

> *We've been through a number of psychologists ... I went to one psychiatrist who just didn't believe it ... [I] decided, no that wasn't going to work for me because he thought that I was not on the spectrum.*

Similarly, Murray explained that he did not talk to others about his relationship:

> *No, only because the best person to talk to is my wife and ... I don't feel like I need to talk to others ... I think naturally Asperger people aren't that keen to talk about their emotions.*

Rachelle shared the long journey that led to her diagnosis:

> *I saw [over] 20 psychologists and psychiatrists and doctors and counsellors etc., etc., trying to work out what was wrong and then finally my son was diagnosed and then I was diagnosed.*

Have The Numbers Gone Nuts?

When NT participants were asked about seeking help, most reported that talking with others was a delicate issue. Many reported that inadequate community knowledge and awareness led to feeling invisible and disbelieved. While they made it clear that they would welcome being able to talk through their difficulties with others, the lack of understanding and resulting opinions and conclusions that others arrived at resulted in mixed reactions. For this reason, many had selected the 'not applicable' option in their survey to the two statements about being believed. Seeking professional help was also reported to cause mixed results. Sophie reported on the difficulties that she encountered from the lack of community understanding:

> *I usually do not [talk about it] because others have no concept of what I go through or deal with. The issues ... of an AS man does not resemble anything from a normal NT – NT relationship for people to relate to. The few times I do reach out ... their response quickly reminds me I shouldn't have reached out to them ... Unless someone has gone through a relationship like ours, there is no way for them to relate to this experience ... I find some friends incredibly judgemental of him, and us, so I retreat further away from them.*

Wanda gave details of the difficulties of explaining the distinct problems:

> *I find when you talk to friends ... or colleagues its more, 'Oh all men are like that' ... You don't really feel that you're listened to or understood ... Other people see your spouse ... his talent and he's able to communicate in a very professional manner to other people, they're just amazing ... and you're like 'you don't live with it' ... Always not believed!*

Complicated Additions

Devastating Judgements

Many ASC and NT participants felt that their experiences were often dismissed or disbelieved. A common outcome of this doubt was that others started to believe the NT person was to blame for the issues in their relationships. NT participants shared that taking on a parental or caretaker role with their autistic partner or family member often reinforced this belief. First, people often judged NT participants negatively when they saw them treating their autistic loved ones in a way that seemed overly parental, almost like they were talking to a 'child'. Second, many NT participants often felt labelled as 'crazy' by their families and others. Sometimes they even felt this way themselves. This feeling came from repeated failed attempts to get their autistic partner to engage in a way that would make the relationship work. Instead, these attempts often ended in frustrating cycles of miscommunication, leading to self-doubt and causing others to think the NT person was at fault.

Parent-child

The majority of NT participants reported that an unpleasant outcome of being placed in a 'caretaker' role in their relationships was the observations and assumptions other people made about their behaviour towards their partner/family members with ASC:

> DAWN *When people observe us as a couple, they think I am treating him like a kid at times ... I know he thinks like that sometimes.*

> SABRINA *If we're not talking business, he's being childlike and I feel like I'm mothering him and I don't*

> *want to be that person ... He tells me ... 'stop trying to be my mother' and I'm like 'stop acting like a 15-year-old', so the conversation is like with a kid.*

QUINN   *And I was telling him this week it almost feels like when I have conversations with him about our relationship it feels like a mum and a child ... I feel it's like a mum is getting onto the child and then the child is trying to do something to kind of calm mum down.*

Notions of irrationality

Reported by the majority of NT participants, another challenging outcome was when seeking help or trying to address issues. They frequently encountered incorrect conclusions from others, as well as their partners and family members, regarding observations and evaluations of their attempts to make sense of their experiences:

RUTH   *It used to be that I was written off as 'emotional', 'crazy', or my thoughts and feelings about things just didn't make sense to him most of the time. Now, he seems to realise that what I say is valid or important more often than he used to.*

HOLLY   *I've had one friend who gave me an absolute lambasting ... and said to me for goodness sake pull yourself together, [your partner is] not the problem, you're the problem ... I'd say such and such – 'Oh my husband does that', and so she just totally wrote off everything I*

Complicated Additions

said ... and so I've chosen not to see her and that's a real sadness because I've lost friends over it.

RONDA   It's extremely hard because any of the dysfunction they see as coming from me ... [My daughter] just threw it back in my face and said 'Oh it's not Asperger's. It's not that at all ... He doesn't even have it. It's you that can't get along with anybody'.

GEORGIA   If these communication issues are really identified and seen that they can have such devastating effects on couples ... I mean just being validated and knowing ... people are starting to realise it's there, it happens, it's real and that the suffering ... whether you call it the Cassandra Phenomenon or some sort of ongoing stress disorder like PTSD ... we do suffer, we suffer as a consequence.

RAE   If you went into a normal counsellor, I'd ... be made the fool, and then they come away more arrogant than ever going 'Well there is nothing wrong with me, it's all you' ... Years ago we went and saw the pastors ... then he just said to both of them 'Oh Rae does talk a lot.' Well, I will never forget it, the two of them just burst out laughing .... you know 'Rae talks so much, she obviously she is just waffling on with gobbledygook' ... It's just hard isn't it; no-one really understands.

Have The Numbers Gone Nuts?

A Disastrous Dynamic

The power struggle between prompting and self-protection led to more layers of communication issues, creating a cycle of back-and-forth conflicts. As each person tried to address their own unmet needs, it resulted in an ongoing pattern of disagreements. This dynamic created a communication tug-of-war in neurodiverse relationships, where neither side truly succeeded. These interactions often became a confusing cycle, sometimes following a predictable path and other times taking unexpected turns. For many ASC and NT participants, this back-and-forth turned into a never-ending communication roundabout, filled with misunderstandings and tension.

The responses from SI 20 (Figure 10.4) and SI 33 (Figure 10.5) revealed some key differences between ASC and NT participants. While many ASC respondents were neutral on these questions, NT respondents largely agreed with the statements. A total of 51% NT participants felt they were not taken seriously, and 68% believed they were not to blame for communication issues. For the ASC group, nearly half (47%) stayed neutral on whether they were responsible for communication difficulties (SI 33). However, 37% did feel they were responsible, while 16% felt they were rarely or never responsible.

Both groups agreed that their communication problems often went unresolved, leading to conversations that just went around in circles without a satisfying outcome (Figures 5.4 in Chapter 5 and 9.1 in Chapter 9). This created a complex system of recurring communication cycles, driven by feelings of not being taken seriously, ongoing misunderstandings and many issues that did not get resolved.

Complicated Additions

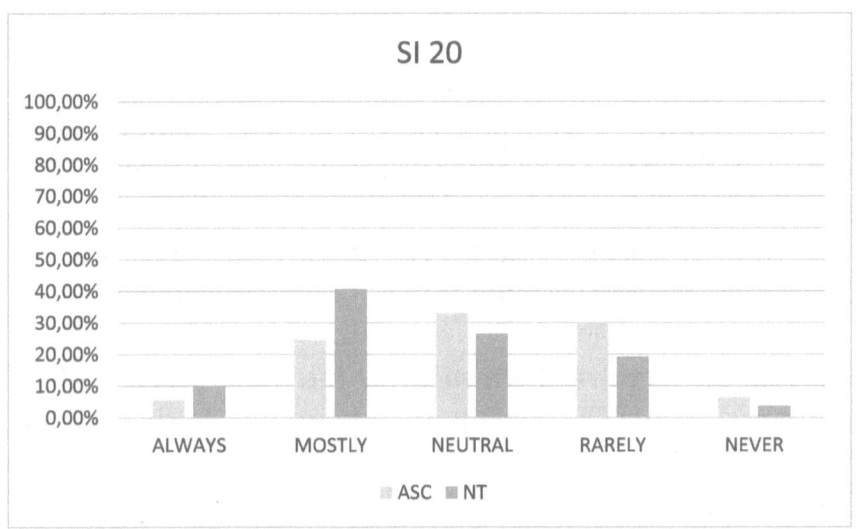

Figure 10.4. SI 20. My ideas are not taken seriously.

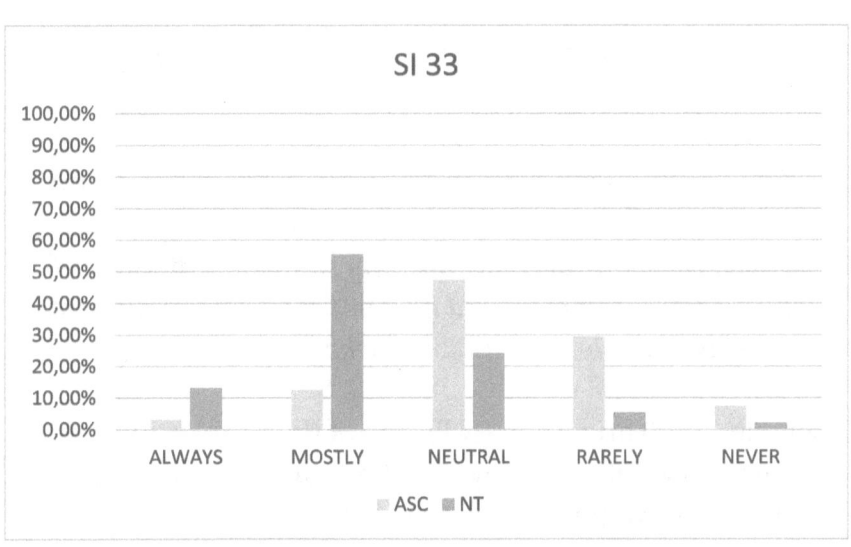

Figure 10.5. SI 33. I am not responsible for most of the communication difficulties.

Have The Numbers Gone Nuts?

While both ASC and NT participants felt that communication was an often unproductive, unresolvable, cyclic situation, each frequently attributed the problems to the other. Sharon's (ASC) comment indicated that other people were the cause:

I guess, in general, people don't like it when other people point out that they are the cause of an ineffective communication.

Despite the fact that the result was often increased conflict, neither ASC or NT participants knew how to discontinue the cycle. Stella (ASC) shared the circular nature of the conversations that she had with her partner:

Difficulties remain ... We raise the same topics over and over again ... We never reach a final conclusion.

Likewise, Sandra (ASC) shared the futility to being caught in the cycle:

I'm saying the same thing over and over because I don't have anything more to maybe say in this situation except you know just saying over and over my side of it so it's kind of is a bit redundant to me and if I don't see it going anywhere it just becomes like I don't know what else to say.

Rachelle (ASC) and Ryan (NT), one of the couples involved in the study, also felt that they could not progress pass a certain point, therefore they had both given up:

RACHELLE *Because what annoys us about each other ... we're beyond the point of bothering to fix them and to try to not do that thing anymore.*

Complicated Additions

RYAN *I'm not sure that going deeper into a conversation would actually resolve anything. We go as deep as we need to go and either there is going to be a resolution or not going to be a resolution. If there is not going to be a resolution there's going to be an argument and a fight and I don't tend to want to go in that territory myself ... She can get quite worked up over a decision that is not going her way ... She has been known to throw things at me in the past too, so I don't tend to want to go into that territory.*

Similarly, most NT participants discussed the unproductive circular characteristics to most of their conversations. Rae lamented the frustration and confusion that resulted:

And you go round and round the mountain and still don't come up with an answer ... but I mean they just tip you over the edge with the frustration and the annoyance and I just think 'why is this so hard'? I can talk, have a conversation with anybody else and everybody else can understand me ... you just get so confused when I try to talk ... I lay it all out there you, still ... are going round and round in circles. People have got no idea, have they?

The Loss of Sense of Self Cycle

The survey data suggested that a common result of the communication un-resolvability and resultant consequences for both NT and ASC people was a sense of a loss of oneself. The interview data revealed that this sense of a loss of oneself was for different reasons between the two groups. A total of 54% of ASC and 55% of NT respondents indicated that they felt this lost sense of self (Figure 10.6).

Have The Numbers Gone Nuts?

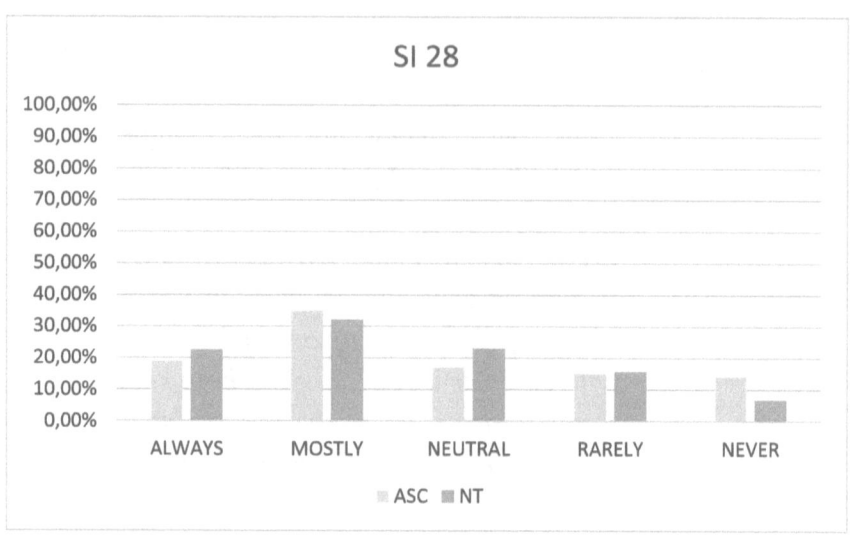

Figure 10.6. SI 28. I feel that I have lost my sense of self (that is, the way I think about and view my personality, beliefs and purpose within the world).

Many ASC participants mentioned how they felt that it was necessary to fit into the neurotypical world, and what that meant to them in their day-to-day lives. When asked to comment on the reason for selecting 'always' or 'mostly' to SI 28 (Figure 10.6), in their survey, the general consensus was an obligation to pretend to be something that they felt they were not.

DANIEL   *For the first half century of my life, I had a sense of purpose - making sense of the world. Then ... I discovered autism. Another decade or so of research and I'm left high and dry - there's no place in the world for adult autistics. We're there, but we conspire to maintain our ignorance.*

Complicated Additions

EDITH   *So I probably identify fairly strongly with myself as an intellectual person because ... I like the way my mind works ... and I know who I am ... With other people I just get lost.*

Rachelle (ASC) and Ryan (NT) shared their individual perspectives on the loss of sense of self, within their relationship with each other:

RACHELLE   *I feel like I'm faking it every day and I can't be the person I want to be ... I just have to conform to what society wants me to be and I can't talk to people the way I want to talk to people. I have to put in all these nice words and use inflection in my voice and try and act normal ... People think I'm rude ... and I'm just surrounded by people who aren't on the spectrum at work and with my husband ... It's like being from another planet, speaking another language and yeah, it's difficult. It's like I wake up every day and when I leave the house I have to put on a mask and pretend ... and when we see other people communicating and smiling at each other and chatting away and stuff and the small talk it's all fake like it's all just nothing, meaningless, we don't find any meaning in it so when we see, it looks meaningless.*

RYAN   *When you are inside the family unit, I feel very much that it is team Rachelle and not team [us] so ... yeah, I do feel like it's the loss of myself, in a lot of ways ... It is really very*

> *much about what she wants, and wants to do, and wants to achieve, and not really much about what I want ... I'm very quick to make a sacrifice ... for the rest of my family ... I'm trying to manage a relationship that all works ... Yes, thinking about others.*

Most NT participants shared that they often felt like they lost their sense of self because they had to constantly give in to the rigid behaviours of their autistic partners or family members. When asked why they chose 'always' or 'mostly' to SI 28 in the survey (Figure 10.6), many said it was due to the sadness and grief they felt over losing the person they used to be.

QUINN — *I no longer know who I am. I think that's probably the most painful part of this whole thing ... I've lost myself ... I love him but I want to get myself back ... I was very outgoing and a 'happy go lucky' kind of girl and I always liked to help people and I felt like I was happy and full in my life and that's not the way I feel anymore ... I have no idea who I am anymore.*

Chapter Synopsis

This chapter focused on the fourth theme 'additional cycles' showing how prompting, relying on prompts and avoiding them can create extra layers of back-and-forth communication. These cycles arise from a power struggle between conflicting needs, which affects how people in neurodiverse relationships interact and impacts everyone involved. The ongoing push and pull between NT participants prompting and ASC participants responding with protective or dependent behaviours added more layers to the communication cycle. These extra cycles often stemmed from differences in emotional connection. Prompting and prompt dependency or prompt avoidance became the primary way of interacting in neurodiverse relationships, with both sides caught in a power struggle to meet their own needs. This ongoing pattern of communication, fuelled by differing emotional needs, became central to how people in neurodiverse relationships related to each other. Unfortunately, it mostly had a negative impact, and even seeking help often ended in frustration. In the next chapter, the fifth theme: 'three potential relationship outcomes' is explored, where three possible outcomes of the communication cycles in neurodiverse relationships are considered.

11

Various Aftermaths

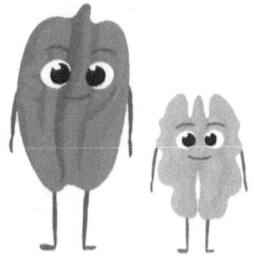

'When we are no longer able to change a situation,
we are challenged to change ourselves.'
Viktor Frankl

Have The Numbers Gone Nuts?

In the two studies it was found that when people with differently wired brains form a relationship together, a unique challenge often emerges. This challenge seems to be linked to certain traits seen in adults with autism. Interestingly, the same patterns were seen across all the neurodiverse relationships studied. These irregularities gradually led to an unconventional way of interacting, which then shaped a distinct dynamic that was consistent across these relationships.

The differing needs for emotional connection, unresolved differences and ongoing communication struggles created a cycle where the person with autism became increasingly dependent on the prompts of the other or avoided them altogether. The resulting dynamic caused multiple difficulties to overcome and often led to a constant state of tension. This dynamic was found to lead to three possible outcomes: the relationship either thrives, simply survives or deteriorates.

Thriving

While not the most common outcome, the data confirmed that outcomes for these relationships can be positive. Survey results show that both groups of participants believe their relationships would improve if they made an effort to listen to each other (Figure 11.1), apologised after disagreements (Figure 11.2) and engaged in meaningful conversations (SI 57; Figure 4.15 in Chapter 4). A total of 50% ASC respondents and 89% of NT respondents agreed that listening to the other person is crucial for good communication (Figure 11.1). Meanwhile, 62% of ASC participants and 57% of NT participants felt that saying sorry is an essential part of maintaining a good relationship (Figure 11.2).

Various Aftermaths

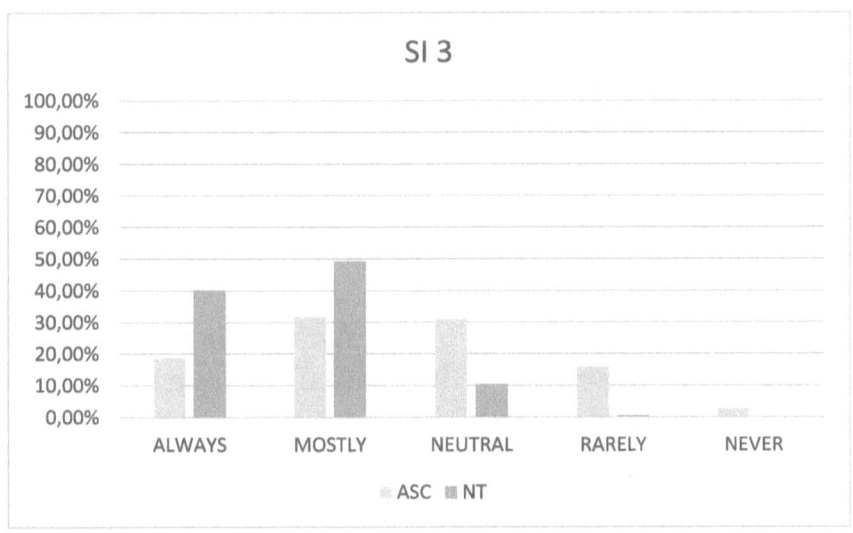

Figure 11.1. SI 3. The best way to get someone to listen to me is to listen to that person first.

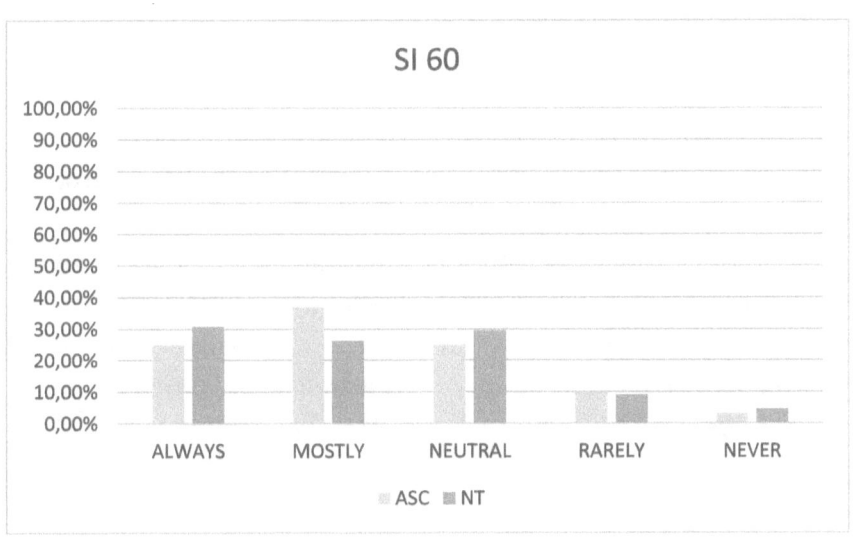

Figure 11.2. SI 60. Our relationship would improve if I apologised when I have hurt my partner/family member's feelings, even if I didn't mean to.

Have The Numbers Gone Nuts?

The survey results revealed that many ASC participants understood the value of listening, having deep conversations and apologising. But, in their interviews, only a few could share real-life examples of putting these practices into action. Those who did, however, showed a willingness to learn about and embrace the differences between ASC and NT individuals. This openness led to positive outcomes in their relationships, proving that understanding each other's unique needs can make a difference. Daniel demonstrated a willingness to learn about his autism, and learn from his partner:

> *Cathy is good at establishing relationships, and works hard at it. We have discovered autism together. She is sympathetic, but her theory of mind doesn't quite grasp the autistic model ... We work hard at being good to each other ... What I know of kindness I have learned from Cathy.*

Similarly, Terry shared how an awareness of the diagnosis and a willingness to learn from his partner helped him:

> *Well, the expectation that I've grown to understand is that I need to actually consciously spend more time with Kim and to further develop my communication skills ... I think I'm doing a lot better than I used to, and being aware of the various conditions that I have, Asperger's diagnosis from about 6 or 7 years ago.*

Matt (ASC) and Mia (NT) shared how Matt had positively responded to the support Mia had provided through her training and how it had helped their relationship to grow:

Various Aftermaths

MATT
> *I've had a lot of training in terms of how to interact with neurotypicals and a lot of practice so Mia and I are actually a long way down the track ... Mia and I may not be your typical AS-NT relationship ... She's really helped me know what it is to do and so now that I'm actually able to do that, our relationship has improved tremendously.*

MIA
> *We do share a good connection in that we talk, we spend time together, it's give and take ... I feel a lot of compassion for how difficult life can be for someone with ASD and I have just total respect for Matt as a person. He's incredibly humble and open to looking at things in his life that he can do better ... It's coming more naturally to him but it's hard ... when you have autism ... Another thing that makes Matt different is his faith ... Yeah, I just feel like we do connect during conversations.*

Likewise, NT participants shared that recognition and acceptance of the diagnosis from both sides made a significant difference to their relationship. Sophie stated this was the case for her:

He recently had his 'ah ha' moment last year in realising he has Asperger's Syndrome. I am incredibly expressive with my emotions and he is able to express himself well too ... The key to making this work between us is clear communication and honesty from both sides.

Equally, Winnie described how awareness of the diagnosis can be transforming:

> *Well, I think from what the women that I have read about, the women that I have met in the group, I am just amazed by (a) their resilience and (b) persistence too, and the hard work they put in to learn and the efforts to make the relationship work and to teach themselves about the condition rather than just walk away.*

Even while appreciating her partner's limitations, Laura shared how cherishing each other, can make a difference:

> *He once or twice has indicated that I, and the home I have created for him, has saved him from despair, but he avoids emotional discussions.*

Surviving

Many ASC and NT participants felt that the differences in their relationships were often too difficult to overcome. When things became unmanageable for them, they experienced a loss of interest in each other, became unresponsive and eventually started to withdraw from the relationship. A total of 52% ASC respondents and 78% NT respondents said they felt pressured to make regretful compromises just to keep the peace (Figure 11.3). Additionally, 46% of ASC participants and 56% of NT participants admitted that trying to communicate often did not feel worth the effort (Figure 11.4).

Various Aftermaths

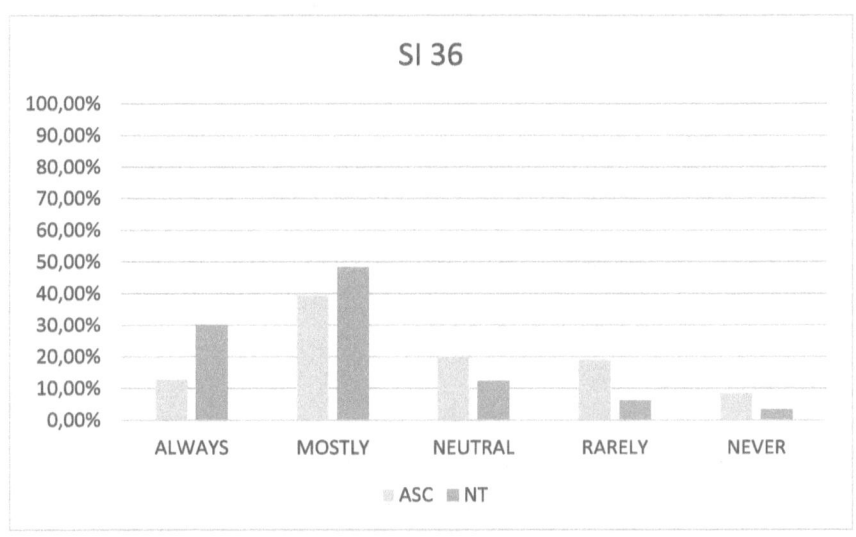

Figure 11.3. SI 36. Regretful compromise is often required to keep the peace.

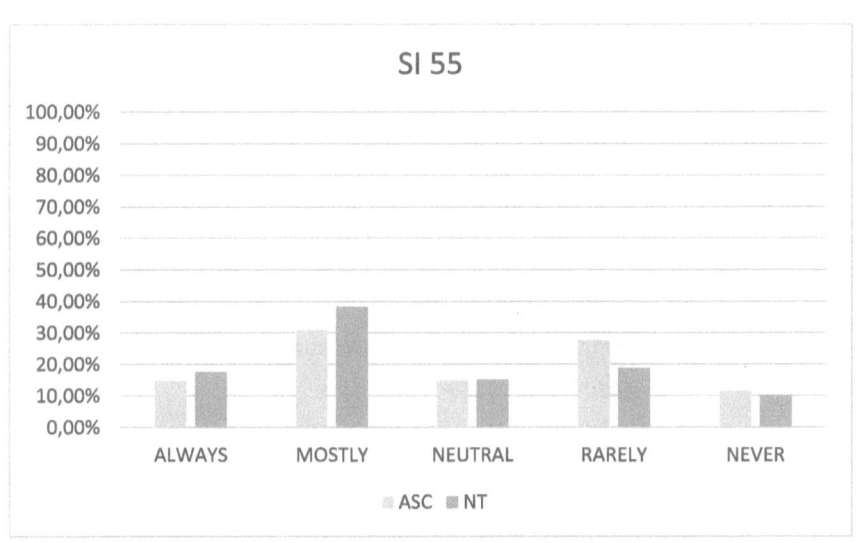

Figure 11.4. SI 55. I have given up trying to communicate because it is not worth the hassle.

Have The Numbers Gone Nuts?

Several participants mentioned that, in private, their relationships felt more like they were merely housemates, even though they appeared to be a 'normal couple' in public. A few even said that, while they stayed in the relationship, they had completely disconnected emotionally from their partner or family member. For many ASC participants, how they managed to keep things going behind closed doors was not discussed; however, Samuel did share how his relationship managed to survive:

> *Our relationship has gone through a lot of upheaval and we separated for a time ... so now we are simply companions ... We do pretty much our own thing apart from the odd thing together ... but affection is really just making each other a cup of tea and coffee and sitting and chatting together, that's about it really.*

In contrast, quite a few NT participants had plenty to say on the subject.

> WANDA   *I've kind of given up ... I think I've kind of worn myself out ... Yeah, I've sort of reached that point of not being hurt anymore and trying not to expect anything and I don't have the answers.*

> HOLLY   *He wasn't responding ... that has caused me to withdraw, not to bother, telling him minor bits of information that are kind of social discourse ... Once we used to chat about the day-to-day things. I just realise quite frequently he's tuned out; he's not receiving.*

Various Aftermaths

MAGGIE   *I won't put myself forward anymore and share as much as I would like to share with him because of his reaction and his unknowing of how to deal with it on an emotional level ... I've heard people say 'Oh look, you've just got to get all your needs met somewhere else with your friends' ... and I thought to myself 'but that's not a marriage'.*

Deteriorating

Many participants expressed disappointment over the collapse of the relationship they had once hoped for, realising that their expectations were no longer possible. To cope with this, some chose to stay in the same house but live completely separate lives, others moved into different homes but continued seeing each other, and a few felt that divorce was their only option. Survey responses from SI 32 (Figure 11.5), SI 56 (Figure 11.6) and SI 53 (Figure 6.10 in Chapter 6) highlight the decline in communication, breakdown of relationships, and in rare cases, instances of physical ill-treatment over time. A total of 43% ASC respondents and 64% NT respondents said that their communication had always or mostly deteriorated (Figure 11.5).

When it came to physical ill-treatment, 61% of ASC respondents said it never happened, while 17% admitted it occurred rarely, 13% said it mostly or always occurred, and 10% were neutral (Figure 11.6). Among NT respondents, 60% said physical ill-treatment never happened, 18% said it rarely occurred, 10% said it mostly or always happened, and 12% chose neutral. Earlier descriptions from SI 53 also show that a significant portion of both ASC and NT participants experienced verbal aggression in their relationships (Figure 6.10 in Chapter 6). About 60% of both groups admitted to dealing with verbal aggression, and 30% of each group acknowledged the presence of physical ill-treatment in their relationships.

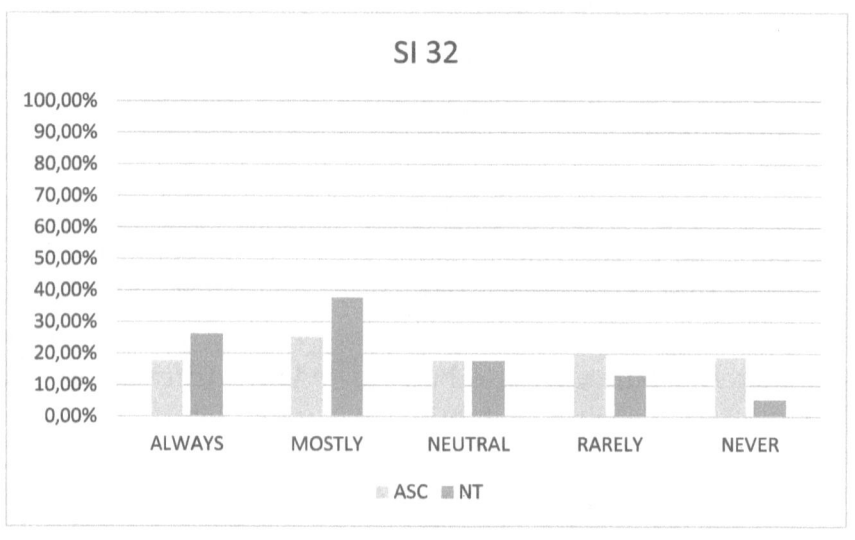

Figure 11.5. SI 32. The quality of our communication has deteriorated over time.

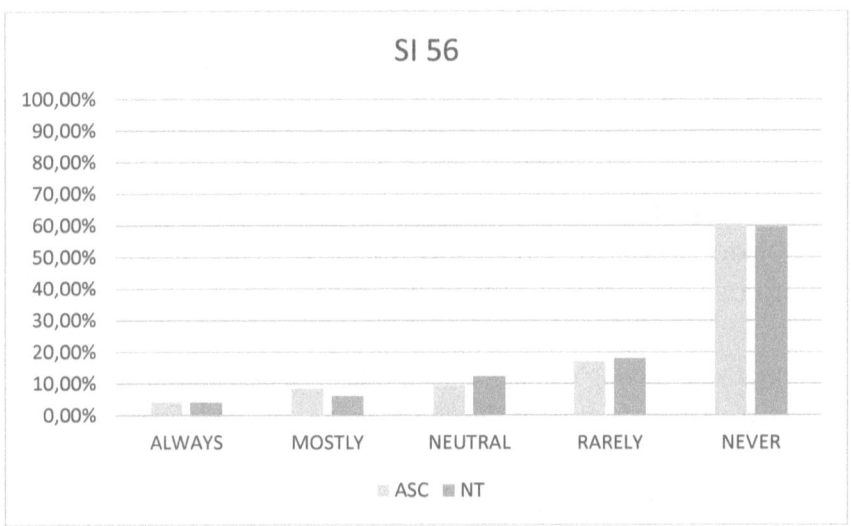

Figure 11.6 SI 56. Frustration triggered by entangled conversation can escalate to physical ill-treatment.

A few participants in the study chose to completely leave their relationships. However, it seems that divorce is relatively rare in neurodiverse relationships. This is often because, once there is an understanding of the condition, people tend to make adjustments to accommodate each other. Unfortunately, sometimes this understanding comes too late to save the relationship. Sharon (ASC), disclosed that her need for solitude ended her marriage:

He understood that I needed some level of solitude, but that took a toll in the marriage eventually.

She went on to give her thoughts on how to save neurodiverse relationships:

Have The Numbers Gone Nuts?

For any relationship to stay strong and go far, they must be allowed to be themselves – AS or NT – and still enjoy the relationship.

Many NT participants reported that they attempted to find unconventional solutions if conventional ones were not an option for them. Tracy had found that a solution for her was to use an empty room in her house:

I just stop talking and leave. I need to protect myself. We now have an empty room in the house, and I can withdraw there.

However, Haley reported that her marriage had ended a few weeks prior to the interview:

I really hope you do get some answers out of it ... how to actually deal with it ... cause, I've ended up, I've left. We've been gone now for about five weeks. So, it's only ... recent, but I did put it to him earlier in the year ... in January, I just said 'Look I'm not happy, I look at you and I think you're not happy as well' ... Like in the end we just stopped talking.

Chapter Synopsis

This chapter illustrated the fifth theme, 'three potential relationship outcomes', which outlined three possible paths for those in neurodiverse relationships dealing with these communication cycles. In the final chapter, the book is summarised by highlighting the key takeaways about the unique dynamics of neurodiverse relationships. The comparison tables that were designed to illustrate similarities and/or differences of survey responses between the males, females are interpreted and summarised. The diagrammatic model that was created based on interview and survey responses is reviewed and we take a look ahead to a future where it is possible to experience a deeper understanding of adult autism and its impact on relationships.

12

Defining Patterns

'The opposite of love is not hate; it's indifference.'
Elie Wiesel

In this final chapter, the study's data and related model (Figure 12.1) will be brought together to explain the findings. Autism is characterised by differences in brain wiring, leading to unique challenges in social skills, repetitive behaviours and verbal and non-verbal communication. The two studies revealed that these challenges often result in a distinctive approach to relationships, which can create a mismatch between autistic and neurotypical individuals. It was discovered that this misalignment triggered specific behaviours and formed distinct communication patterns.

The data highlighted that extensive differences in needs, expectations, and abilities between people in neurodiverse relationships frequently lead to prompt dependency behaviours. When ASC individuals avoid or are unresponsive to reciprocal interactions, emotional connection diminishes. This often triggers NT individuals to seek connection through prompting, which can lead to either dependency or avoidance from ASC individuals. Over time, these interactions form a cycle of prompt dependency, with negative effects for both parties, particularly NT individuals, who often feel the impact most strongly.

Neurotypical individuals typically desire deeper emotional connection and reciprocal interactions, while ASC individuals, facing communication challenges and differing emotional needs, may struggle to meet these expectations. The resulting dynamic creates emotional gaps, compelling NT individuals to prompt for the connection they seek. However, this cycle of prompting, dependence and avoidance perpetuates discord, with both parties unable to fully meet each other's needs.

These cycles were shown to have significant negative effects on both ASC and NT individuals, often leading to frustration and additional interaction patterns that further strain relationships. Despite the variety of relationships examined (romantic, familial or sibling) the findings revealed a common thread: all individuals desire emotional connection and mutual understanding. However, when ASC individuals avoid emotional interactions, NT individuals may feel unfulfilled, intensifying the cycle of unmet needs and discord. Over time, these patterns compound, creating persistent challenges in neurodiverse relationships.

The Numbers Narrative

The graphs and tables from the survey confirm what the interviews revealed. The extensive differences between autistic and neurotypical people significantly affect their relationships. Also, the ways in which each handle these differences remain consistent because the contrasts between autistic and neurotypical individuals are a permanent part of who they are. The two studies show that these patterns remain consistent in autistic-neurotypical relationships everywhere.

The tables were designed to show the differences and similarities between males and females in each group, as well as patterns within and between the groups. One key takeaway is that autistic females are quite different from neurotypical females, as they tend to face social and communication challenges similar to autistic males. Interestingly, the tables also reveal that neurotypical males have more in common with neurotypical females than with autistic males. However, the tables do not explain why these differences exist. Combining the study's statistics with interview insights and prior research can help to piece together a clearer narrative.

The studies by Kock et al. (2019) and Tantam et al. (2019) discovered that autistic women often struggle to understand or respond to the subtle non-verbal cues in relationships. Their research showed that these challenges were often tied to the unpredictable and unique nature of relationships, as well as the lack of clear 'rules' to follow. Likewise, Müller et al. (2008) found that both men and women with autism talked about having trouble deciphering their partner's intentions and admitted that they both often overlooked verbal and non-verbal communication. In my studies, Rachelle (ASC) described these types of difficulties:

This is just what relationships are to me, full of misunderstandings and expectations that I have no idea what they expect.

Have The Numbers Gone Nuts?

Similar to what many ASC males reported, Sharon (ASC) preferred time alone:

> *In my previous marriage to NT-partner, I have found that our expectations and requirements for emotional connection were quite different. I was craving more personal space and time, while he was wanting to do many things together.*

Perhaps these similarities between ASC males and females are due to Baron-Cohen's (1997) 'extreme male brain' theory which proposes that autistic people of both sexes have brains that are more masculine than expected. Ryan (NT) had a lot to say about this aspect:

> *I mean being female and being Aspie ... in one way it is actually a good part of Rachelle being Aspie in that she has a very male, I mean I know Simon Baron-Cohen talks a lot about Asperger's being extreme maleness ... that actually has a bit of value as well in that she tries to think logically ... she is quite sort of very masculine the way she sees things, the way she does things, she's comfortable around males, she is more comfortable around males than she is around females, she doesn't play the inter-personal games that you see females in groups playing with each other and she doesn't understand them at all, and that's one of the reasons why she struggles a bit at work sometimes, cause she's often puts her technical ability ... above other people ... and she struggles to intuit what the unspoken communications are between staff members and her, and it's tricky for her to do that, and so that's expected of a guy. Women will expect a male manager not to have that skill set ... It's positive in that it is easier to have a more equal relationship ... but also it is a negative in that she can overstep the mark a lot in that*

she sees herself as being more equal than me, but usually you have two people and people with two different agendas and in a partnership, you usually amalgamate that agenda to an agreed upon agenda to work off. She is not very good at that. Compromise and negotiation are not things she thinks to involve herself with. She doesn't understand why what 'she wants' shouldn't be what 'we want.' Whereas with me, I am quite strong in neurotypical in a lot of ways. For me, I mull things over. I think about things. I look at other aspects to it, even I might sit on it before coming to a decision about something but she makes a decision quite quickly and acts on it.

Or perhaps it is about gender identity as several studies show that autistic people are more likely than neurotypical people to be gender diverse. According to Peachey and Crane (2024) 'people who are nonbinary do not feel like men or women. They might feel like a mix of both, or like they have no gender at all. Autistic people are more likely than non-autistic people to be nonbinary' (p. 462). Van Der Miesen et al. (2016) suggested that a consequence of difficulties in social interactions could lead to gender dysphoria. Perhaps it is a combination of these aspects. According to the extreme male brain theory, prenatal testosterone may not only lead to a higher disposition towards ASC, but also gender dysphoria, as an expression of extreme male characteristics (Van Der Miesen et al., 2016).

Although there are several similarities in how autism presents in males and females, research shows there are some differences. A study by Driver and Chester (2021) suggests that females tend to have fewer social and communication challenges compared to males. Similarly, Allely (2019a) found that females with autism often show stronger social skills or seem to adapt better socially than their male counterparts. According to Tony Attwood, autistic females can have higher levels of emotional empathy but may avoid emotional conversations because they feel overwhelmed or 'emotionally contaminated' by others' negative emotions. Based on his experience and research, he explains that this 'emotional contamination' comes from their heightened sensitivity to others' moods, which can leave them unsure of how to respond or help someone feel better.

These differences might also be linked to camouflaging, which Cage and Troxell-Whitman (2020) describe as hiding an autistic identity by adopting non-autistic behaviours in social situations. Their research suggests that people who strongly identify as autistic are less likely to camouflage if they have openly shared their identity with others. Embracing and disclosing their autism can make it easier to stop masking their traits. For girls and women with autism, the story is often different. They may feel more pressure to develop strategies that help them appear 'socially typical'. Jamison et al. (2017) found that, in general, girls, whether neurotypical or autistic, tend to develop social skills faster than boys. Allely (2019a, 2019b) observed that autistic females often learn to mimic socially acceptable behaviours to blend in and avoid standing out. This faster social development can make challenges less noticeable early on, leading to girls on the spectrum being underdiagnosed. However, as they grow older and face higher social expectations, their struggles often become more apparent. For girls who are not diagnosed until later in life, the lack of early interventions and support can lead to serious internal challenges, such as anxiety or depression, which may appear as the main issue instead of their underlying autism.

Defining Patterns

Even with the small number of neurotypical males included in my studies, the tables show that neurotypical males are more alike with neurotypical females in the area of interpersonal communication than with autistic males. Similar to neurotypical females, neurotypical males seem to want more emotional connection than they typically get from an autistic partner or family member. Alex (NT) described how he would like more connection in his relationship with Mary (ASC):

Let's do something together or communicate, go somewhere or do something and let's build a more of a romantic situation ... she is just not hardwired to naturally be that way. So, I think she just feels guilty for that. But it is more, when I say romance that could just be going to dinner, or anything you know, ... I would like a bit more ... she is not romantic ... I feel like I am missing out on something. I have this feeling that I don't really understand ... why am I in this relationship? You know, I doubt myself and I think why aren't I just going down the other road. You know, being in a normal relationship.

An anonymous male NT survey respondent said:

I deliberately don't think a lot about how much emotional warmth I would like in our relationship, because it's not going to happen ... Why torment myself? It's better to get on with life and learn how to make it work as best we can.

Ryan (NT) pointed out how he handled the lack of connection with his ASC wife:

She will actually present being Aspie as being a superiority ... I've got to the point now where I don't try and, I actually keep her somewhat from my circle of friends so I don't lose my friends ... I am involved with a lot of community events and organisations so I get a lot of my social life enough through being involved with Rotary, or being involved with a voluntary community service organisation and those type of areas where I like to do stuff in the community. That's where I get my social interaction.

However, the reasons for seeking connection might differ between neurotypical males and females. Tony Attwood suggests that males tend to seek emotional connection more for reassurance and affirmation rather than for shared emotional support. Irrespective of the reason the tables show that while there are some differences, neurotypical males are quite similar to neurotypical females in their need for connection.

Additionally, the tables show that autistic females and males are quite similar to each other. These differences and similarities are yet to be fully understood. More research is required to answer the questions that still remain.

Constructive Considerations

The results shown in the tables and graphs together with the participants words not only highlight some of the unique dynamics within neurodiverse relationships but also pave the way for understanding how distinctive neurodiverse relationships are. Understanding the many differences will facilitate positive outcomes that can arise when these relationships are nurtured with awareness and support.

Defining Patterns

An important consideration for people in neurodiverse relationships is to find ways to escape the hold of the communication cycle that forms in these relationships. Through gaining knowledge about each other's needs, expectations and abilities it is possible to reduce the cycles' impacts. While the information contained in the *'Have They Gone Nuts'* 3-book series can go some way towards gaining this knowledge, it is important to remember that each person is different, so what works for one, may not work for another. However, the findings from these studies, combined with other research shows that there are some similarities in the unconventionalities that form in neurodiverse relationships and these similarities can be used to gain the knowledge needed to find ways to move out of the negative aspects of the cycle.

This can be achieved through gaining understanding, effective communication and mutual respect. Education about each person's neurotype is foundational. Learning about differences in thinking, communication and behaviour fosters empathy and reduces misunderstandings. Embracing each other's unique perspectives, such as heightened attention to detail or creative problem-solving, enriches the relationship and highlights its strengths.

Effective communication is essential for navigating neurodiverse dynamics. Using clear, direct language and allowing space to express needs, boundaries and preferences helps prevent misinterpretations. People in neurodiverse relationships should strive for open discussions and adapt communication styles to meet each other's needs. Additionally, practising empathy and patience strengthens the connection. Each may need time to process thoughts, while individuals

Have The Numbers Gone Nuts?

with ASC may have different sensory sensitivities or communication styles. Patience allows both to feel heard and respected.

Flexibility in problem-solving is another key aspect of successful neurodiverse relationships. Creative and adaptive approaches to challenges help each find solutions that work for both. Respecting each other's autonomy and individuality is equally important, ensuring a balance between shared quality time and space for personal interests.

Social skills training can be beneficial for individuals with ASC, helping them navigate social situations and better understand social cues. NT people can support this process by acting as social advocates or 'social secretaries'. Similarly, advocacy and accommodations play a vital role. NT people can assist in advocating for workplace adjustments or other accommodations, improving the quality of life for their ASC counterparts.

Education about neurodiverse relationships also addresses broader societal issues. Promoting awareness helps break down stigmas and reduces misconceptions about neurodivergence. By embracing differences and fostering inclusivity, we create supportive environments in schools, workplaces and social settings. This advocacy extends to challenging discriminatory practices and promoting policies that amplify the voices of neurodiverse communities.

Finally, the unique dynamics of neurodiverse relationships require intentionality and care. Building empathy, respecting individual needs and embracing differences lead to healthier, more supportive partnerships. By investing in education and

Defining Patterns

fostering mutual understanding, neurodiverse relationships can thrive.

Drawing Conclusions

The model (Figure 12.1) from these studies illustrates what the data is saying. Specifically, it highlights both challenges and opportunities in neurodiverse relationships. While it shows many difficult outcomes, it also identifies some positive possibilities, which could be valuable for neurodiverse individuals, counsellors and researchers.

It begins with the need for neurotypical individuals to experience healthy, reciprocal relationships, built on meaningful conversations, companionship and intimacy. However, these needs are often unmet due to the social interaction difficulties faced by their autistic partners or family members. Instead, individuals with ASC often need to escape social situations and seek solitude through non-social activities as a way to cope with these interaction challenges.

At this point, two main patterns emerge. The first pattern is driven by NT adults trying to improve interactions and strengthen their connection with their ASC partners or family members. They may encourage more involvement or try to fulfill their need for a deeper relationship. Sometimes these efforts succeed, but often the ASC individual either avoids these attempts or does not respond. This avoidance can lead to more frequent prompting from the NT person, creating a cycle. Because occasional success reinforces the prompting behaviour, this cycle becomes hard to break. Over time, the back-and-forth of NT prompting and ASC avoidance or selective responses forms a continuous loop of dependency on prompts or protective withdrawal.

The second pathway stems from the ASC individual's need for social disengagement. This need affects and feeds into the cycles mentioned earlier. Challenges such as not asking questions, misunderstanding actions or making incorrect assumptions further reduce meaningful conversations. This, in turn, intensifies the cycle of prompting, avoidance and reliance on prompts. Over time, NT partners or family members may take on more of a parental or caretaker role, leaving both parties unable to meet their core needs.

The model also shows additional interaction patterns that arise from unmet needs and power struggles. These include the cycles: 'imitating normalcy', 'stonewalling', 'seeking help' and 'loss of self'. These cycles often occur alongside and influence the primary cycles of prompt dependency and self-protectiveness. All these cycles are interconnected, shaping the dynamics of the relationship and influencing its trajectory. Finally, the model identifies three possible outcomes from these interaction cycles, showing how they might evolve.

The challenges of getting stuck in the prompt dependency cycle can be discouraging, but there is hope. With more research into neurodiverse relationship dynamics, we can break this cycle and create meaningful, supportive connections between autistic and neurotypical partners and families. By empowering individuals with the right knowledge and tools, we open the door to deeper understanding, healthier communication, and more fulfilling relationships. This model, along with the insights shared in this series of books has the potential to be fundamental information —not

Defining Patterns

just for counsellors and therapists, but for neurodiverse couples and families seeking to navigate their differences with confidence, reduce communication struggles and build relationships that truly thrive.

Have The Numbers Gone Nuts?

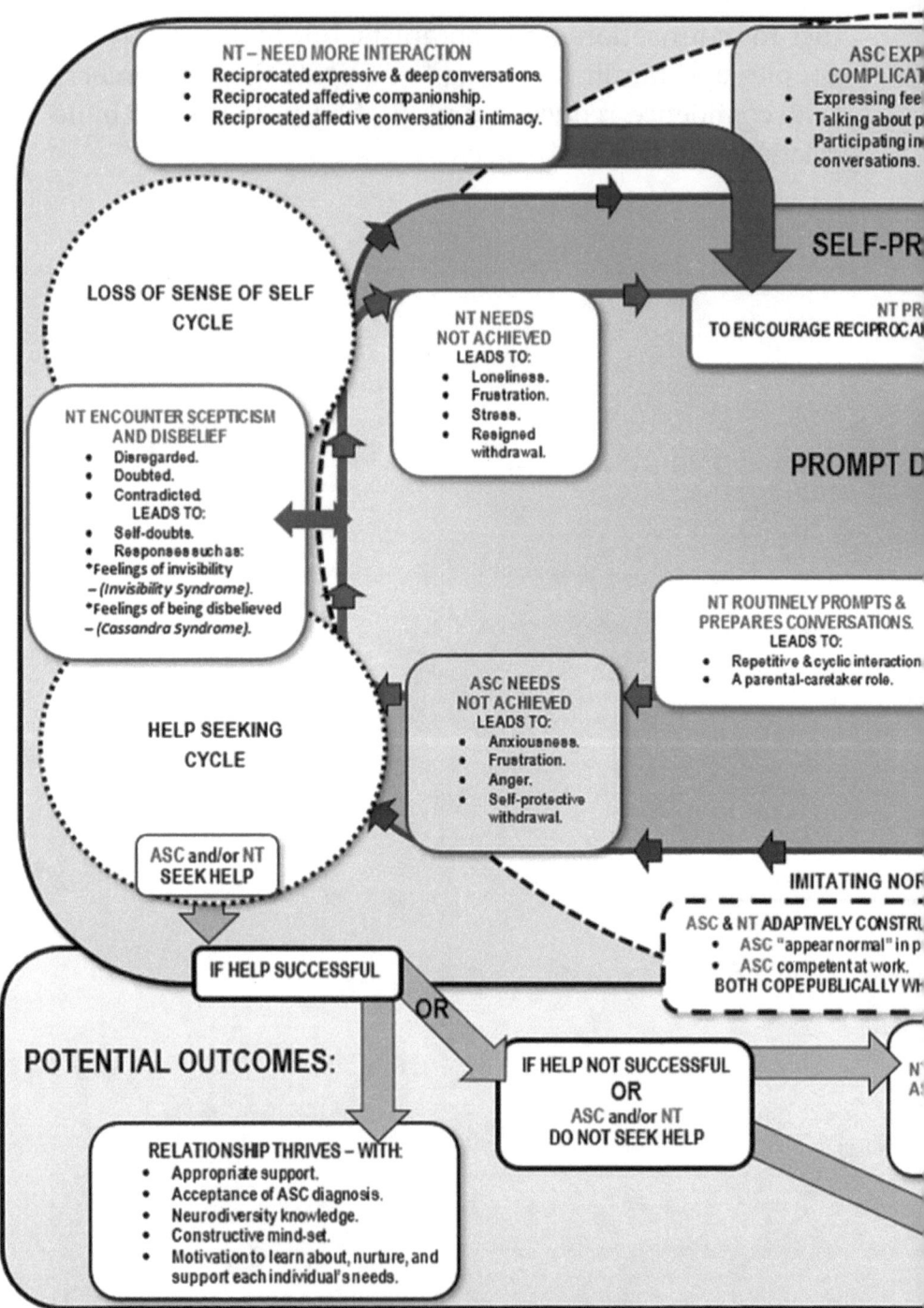

Figure 12.1. Prompt Dependency Cycle with Interwoven Additional

Defining Patterns

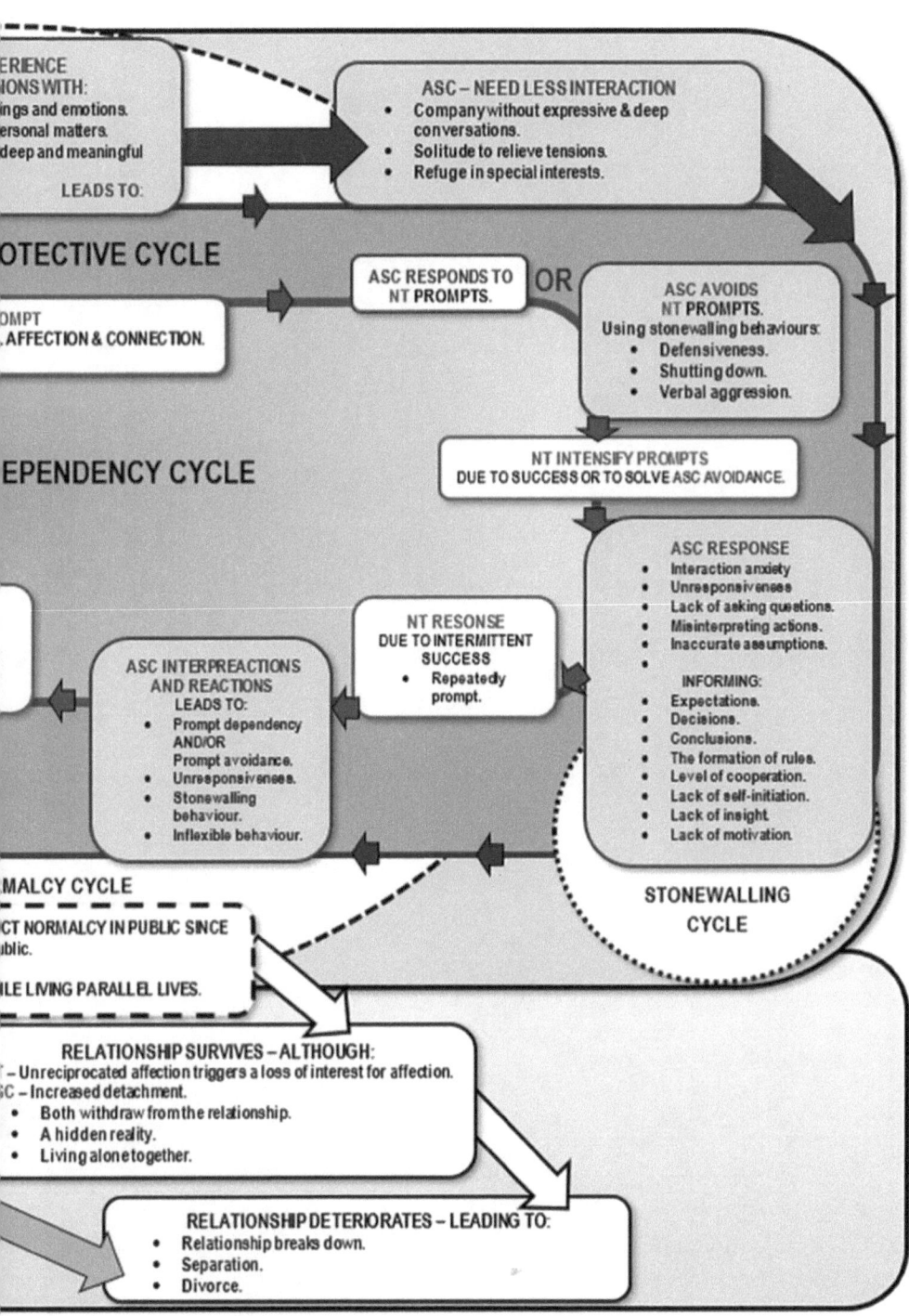

Cycles and Potential Outcomes

Dr Bronwyn Maree Wilson

is a teacher, researcher and author who is passionate about diversity and inclusion. Her work with students in the classroom led her to embark on globally-renowned research on neurodiverse relationships, that sees her now help adults across the world increase their understanding of each other and their differences to achieve better outcomes.

After completing a Bachelor of Education at James Cook University, Townsville, a Master of Special Education at Griffith University, Brisbane and her PhD at Edith Cowan University, Perth, Bronwyn has authored articles and published her research findings in peer-reviewed papers. She has also published her theses, and has now turned her research into a book, the first in a three-part series on neurodiverse relationships.

Bronwyn has presented her research findings at the 5th Asia Pacific Austism Conference in 2017 and the 5th World Austism Conference in the USA in 2018.

As a wife, mother, daughter and sibling of people on the autism spectrum, Bronwyn's life experiences have underpinned the way she approached the research process. Rather than purely conforming to conventional interview methods, chatting, and talking over many hours with her participants created a relaxed dialogue that delivered rare insights into their lives.

An engaging and relatable speaker, Bronwyn connects to audiences both big and small.

She is available to speak to small groups, support groups, organisations and conferences on:

The Unique Challenges of Neurodiverse Relationships

- Big Differences, Big Complications.
- A Hidden Life on Different Pages.
- Difficult Concepts to Convey.
- Contrasting Needs, Contrasting Responses.

The Dynamic System of Communication in Neurodiverse Relationships

- Circular Conversation.
- A Dynamic Communication System.
- A Caretaker Role.
- Controversial Cassandra.

Essential Strategies for Positive Outcomes in Neurodiverse Relationships

- The Good and Bad of Support.
- The Need to Grow Neurodiversity Knowledge.
- Finding the Goldilocks Zone.
- Cultivating Appreciation.

For more details or to book email Bronwyn at arae@bronwilson.com   www.bronwilson.com

About the Author

Bronwyn Wilson lives in a small beachside town in Western Australia, after moving from Queensland for her husband's work. Following a career in teaching she embarked on research, completing a PhD thesis at Edith Cowan University, Perth, Western Australia, researching the communication difficulties that can occur within the close relationships of adults with ASD Level 1 (Asperger's Syndrome). Bronwyn also holds a Master of Special Education, obtained from Griffith University, Brisbane, and a Bachelor of Education, obtained from James Cook University, Townsville.

She has published peer-reviewed papers and presented at the 5th Asia Pacific Autism Conference in 2017 held at the International Convention Centre in Sydney, and at the 5th World Autism Conference, Houston, Texas, USA in 2018. Today, Bronwyn works as an online sessional tutor at Edith Cowan University while also authoring books and

Have The Numbers Gone Nuts?

journal articles. She enjoys swimming most days, sewing and decorating her home, along with watching the boats go past, listening to the waves and enjoying the ocean views from her verandah.

Acknowledgements

I express my sincere gratitude to each of my supervisors who supported me in my studies – Dr Wendi Beamish and Dr Steve Hay in the first, and Dr Susan Main, Dr John O'Rourke and Dr Deslea Konza in the second. Their professional and personal commitment, and their input and feedback, assisted in the realisation of research that I am honoured to have accomplished. Their valuable support has contributed to raising awareness of the unseen struggles of the population of people whose life challenges were explored in these studies.

A special mention goes to Professor Tony Attwood; a wise and knowledgeable supporter of my research journey, who, over quite a few years, has watched my personal and professional growth, while encouraging the development of my understanding of neurodiverse relationships.

I also thank God, who keeps me in His safe hands through all my dark hours (and there's been many), leading me through the circumstances and experiences that have allowed me to embark on this journey. After completing my first study, He kept me persisting through the second, to see them to their conclusions and then to authoring this book.

And lastly, but not at all least, I wish to thank all my participants who opened their lives to me with such forthrightness and honesty. They joined with me under a common cause, and willingly shared a part of themselves. Their collaboration, together with, the quality of data their candid input provided and contributions to the survey data, have worked together to give the studies and this associated book, depth and strength of meaning to make these projects the best that they could be.

My aspiration for this book is enhancement of knowledge regarding neurodiverse relationships in the wider community. The hope is that the understanding of those who provide the services, the programs, and the support, will be augmented, so they are better able to accomplish what they do best. The dream is to see an improvement in the lives, and a decline in the challenges faced, of those in neurodiverse relationships around the world.

References

Addabbo, T., Sarti, E., & Sciulli, D. (2016). Healthy life, social interaction and disability. *Quality and Quantity, 50*(6), 2609-2623. https://doi.org/10.1007/s11135-015-0279-9

Ainsworth, K., Robertson, A. E., Welsh, H., Day, M., Watt, J., Barry, F., Stanfield, A., & Melville, C. (2020). Anxiety in adults with autism: Perspectives from practitioners. *Research in Autism Spectrum Disorders, 69*. https://doi.org/10.1016/j.rasd.2019.101457

Allely, C. S. (2019a). Exploring the female autism phenotype of repetitive behaviours and restricted interests (RBRIs): a systematic PRISMA review. *Advances in Autism, 5*(3), 171-186. https://doi.org/10.1108/AIA-09-2018-0030

Allely, C. S. (2019b). Understanding and recognising the female phenotype of autism spectrum disorder and the "camouflage" hypothesis: a systematic PRISMA review. *Advances in Autism, 5*(1), 14-37. https://doi.org/10.1108/AIA-09-2018-0036

Amaral, D. G. (2017). Examining the causes of autism. *Cerebrum : the Dana forum on brain science, 2017*, cer-01-17. https://pubmed.ncbi.nlm.nih.gov/28698772 https://www.ncbi.nlm.nih.gov/pmc/articles/PMC5501015/

Anon. (2020). Raising awareness of the impact of autism in long-term intimate adult relationships in Australia (S. C. o. A. 2020, Trans.). In *(Vol. 12, pp. 1-4)*. Select Committee on Autism 2020.

Arad, P. (2020). *When your man is on the spectrum: To know, understand and transform your relationship*. Independently published.

Arad, P., Shechtman, Z., & Attwood, T. (2022). Physical and mental well-being of women in neurodiverse relationships: A comparative study. *Journal of Psychology & Psychotherapy, 12*(1), 1-9.

Ariyo, A. M., & Mgbeokwii, G. N. (2019). Perception of companionship in relation to marital satisfaction : a study of married men and women. *IFE PsychologIA : An International Journal, 27*(1), 1-8.

Aston, M. (2001). *The other half of Asperger Syndrome. A guide to living in a relationship with a partner who has Asperger Syndrome*. The National Autistic Society.

Aston, M. (2003). *Aspergers in love. Couple relationships and family affairs*. Jessica Kingsley Publishers.

Attwood, T. (2007). *The complete guide to Asperger's Syndrome*. Jessica Kingsley Publishers.

Attwood, T. (2015). *The complete guide to Asperger's Syndrome* (Revised ed.). Jessica Kingsley Publishers.

Bambara, L. M., Cole, C. L., & Thomas, A. (2021). Linking peer-mediated interventions to address conversational difficulties in adolescents with autism. *Perspectives of*

References

the ASHA Special Interest Groups, 6(1), 55-68. https://doi.org/10.1044/2020_PERSP-20-00151

Baron-Cohen, S. (2015). ASD vs. ASC: Is one small letter important? Grand Ballroom B (Grand America Hotel).

Baron-Cohen, S., & Hammer, J. (1997). Is autism an extreme form of the "male brain"? *Advances in Infancy Research, 11,* 193-217.

Baron-Cohen, S., Knickmeyer, R. C., & Belmonte, M. K. (2005). Sex differences in the brain: Implications for explaining autism. *Science, 310*(5749), 819-819-823. https://www.jstor.org/stable/3842756

Baumeister, R. F., & Leary, M. R. (1995). The need to belong: Desire for interpersonal attachments as a fundamental human motivation. *Psychological Bulletin, 117*(3), 497-529. https://doi.org/10.1037/0033-2909.117.3.497

Bentley, K. (2007). *Alone together. Making an Asperger marriage work.* Jessica Kingsley Publishers.

Bishop-Fitzpatrick, L., Mazefsky, C. A., Eack, S. M., & Minshew, N. J. (2017). Correlates of social functioning in autism spectrum disorder: The role of social cognition. *Research in Autism Spectrum Disorders, 35,* 25-34. https://doi.org/10.1016/j.rasd.2016.11.013

Bostock-Ling, J. S. (2017). *Life satisfaction of neurotypical women in intimate relationship with a partner who has Asperger's Syndrome: An exploratory study.* University of Sydney.

Bostock-Ling, J. S., Cumming, S. R., & Bundy, A. (2012). Life satisfaction of neurotypical women in intimate relationship with an Asperger's Syndrome partner: A systematic review of the literature. *Journal of Relationships Research, 3*(201212), 95-105. https://doi.org/10.1007/s10803-008-0541-2

Braden, B. B., Smith, C. J., Thompson, A., Glaspy, T. K., Wood, E., Vatsa, D., Abbott, A. E., McGee, S. C., & Baxter, L. C.

(2017). Executive function and functional and structural brain differences in middle-age adults with autism spectrum disorder. *Autism Research, 10*(12), 1945-1959. https://doi.org/10.1002/aur.1842

Brown, L. H., Silvia, P. J., Myin-Germeys, I., & Kwapil, T. R. (2007). When the need to belong goes wrong: The expression of social anhedonia and social anxiety in daily life. *Psychological Science, 18*(9), 778-782. https://doi.org/10.1007/s10648-021-09633-6

Bruce, H., Munday, K., & Kapp, S. K. (2023). Exploring the experiences of autistic transgender and non-binary adults in seeking gender identity health care. *Autism in Adulthood, 5*(2), 191-203.

Cage, E., & Troxell-Whitman, Z. (2020). Understanding the relationships between autistic identity, disclosure, and camouflaging. *Autism Adulthood, 2*(4), 334-338. https://doi.org/10.1089/aut.2020.0016

Canevello, A., & Crocker, J. (2010). Creating good relationships: Responsiveness, relationship quality, and interpersonal goals. *Journal of Personality and Social Psychology, 99*(1), 78-106. https://doi.org/10.1037/a0018186

Caruana, N., McArthur, G., Woolgar, A., & Brock, J. (2017). Simulating social interactions for the experimental investigation of joint attention. *Neuroscience & Biobehavioral Reviews, 74*(Part A), 115-125. https://doi.org/https://doi.org/10.1016/j.neubiorev.2016.12.022

Cridland, E. K., Jones, S. C., Magee, C. A., & Caputi, P. (2014). Family-focused autism spectrum disorder research: A review of the utility of family systems approaches. *Autism, 18*(3), 213-222. https://doi.org/10.1177/1362361312472261

Deisinger, J. (2011). History of autism spectrum disorders. In *History of special education: Advances in special education* (Vol.

References

21, pp. 237-267). Emerald Group Publishing Limited. https://doi.org/10.1108/S0270-4013(2011)0000021013

Domingue, R., & Mollen, D. (2009). Attachment and conflict communication in adult romantic relationships. *Journal of Social and Personal Relationships, 26*(5), 678-696.

Donovan, A. P. A., & Basson, M. A. (2017). The neuroanatomy of autism - a developmental perspective. *Journal of Anatomy, 230*(1), 4-15. https://doi.org/10.1111/joa.12542

Driver, B., & Chester, V. (2021). The presentation, recognition and diagnosis of autism in women and girls. *Advances in Autism, 7*(3), 194-207. https://doi.org/10.1108/AIA-12-2019-0050

Dubin, N. (2009). *Asperger Syndrome and anxiety*. Jessica Kingsley Publishers.

Egan, V., & Linenberg, O. (2019). The measurement of adult pathological demand avoidance traits. *Journal of Autism and Developmental Disorders, 49*(2), 481-494. https://doi.org/10.1007/s10803-018-3722-7

Ekman, E., & Hiltunen, A. J. (2015). Modified CBT using visualization for Autism Spectrum Disorder (ASD), anxiety and avoidance behavior - a quasi-experimental open pilot study. *Scandinavian Journal of Psychology, 56*(6), 641-648.

Elder, J., & Thomas, M. (2006). *Different like me: My book of autism heroes*. Jessica Kingsley. http://catdir.loc.gov/catdir/toc/ecip0512/2005014169.html

Finkel, E. J., Simpson, J. A., & Eastwick, P. W. (2017). The psychology of close relationships: Fourteen core principles. *Annual Review of Psychology, 68*(1), 383-411.

Fletcher-Watson, S., Leekam, S. R., & Findlay, J. M. (2013). Social interest in high-functioning adults with Autism Spectrum Disorders. *Focus on Autism and Other Developmental Disabilities, 28*(4), 222-229. https://doi.org/10.1177/1088357613480829

Fortunato, A., Giovanardi, G., Innocenzi, E., Mirabella, M., Caviglia, G., Lingiardi, V., & Speranza, A. M. (2022). Is It autism? A critical commentary on the co-occurrence of Gender Dysphoria and Autism Spectrum Disorder. *Journal of Homosexuality*, 69(7), 1204-1221. https://doi.org/10.1080/00918369.2021.1905385

Gillberg, C., Gillberg, I. C., Thompson, L., Biskupsto, R., & Billstedt, E. (2015). Extreme ("pathological") demand avoidance in autism: a general population study in the Faroe Islands. *European Child & Adolescent Psychiatry*, 24(8), 979-984. https://doi.org/10.1007/s00787-014-0647-3

Grigg, C. (2012). *ASPIA's handbook for partner support: A collection of ASPIA's best information for the support of partners of adults with Asperger's Syndrome.* Carol Grigg. www.aspia.org.au

Grzadzinski, R., Huerta, M., & Lord, C. (2013). DSM-5 and autism spectrum disorders (ASDs): an opportunity for identifying ASD subtypes. *Molecular Autism*, 4(1), 1-6. https://doi.org/10.1186/2040-2392-4-12

Hancock, G., Stokes, M. A., & Mesibov, G. (2019). Differences in romantic relationship experiences for individuals with an autism spectrum disorder. *Sexuality and Disability.* https://doi.org/10.1007/s11195-019-09573-8

Howlin, P., & Magiati, I. (2017). Autism spectrum disorder: Outcomes in adulthood. *Current Opinion in Psychiatry*, 30(2), 69. https://doi.org/10.1097/YCO.0000000000000308

Jacobs, B. (2006). *Loving Mr Spock. Undertsanding an aloof lover. Could it be Asperger's Syndrome?* Jessica Kingsley Publishers.

James, I. (2005). *Asperger's Syndrome and high achievement : Some very remarkable people.* Jessica Kingsley Publishers. https://ebookcentral.proquest.com/lib/ECU/detail.action?docID=290867

References

Jamison, R., Bishop, S. L., Huerta, M., & Halladay, A. K. (2017). The clinician perspective on sex differences in autism spectrum disorders. *Autism, 21*(6), 772-784. https://doi.org/10.1177/1362361316681481

Jaswal, V. K., & Akhtar, N. (2019). Being versus appearing socially uninterested: Challenging assumptions about social motivation in autism. *Behavioral and Brain Sciences, 42*, e82, Article e82. https://doi.org/10.1017/S0140525X18001826

Jenkinson, R., Milne, E., & Thompson, A. (2020). The relationship between intolerance of uncertainty and anxiety in autism: A systematic literature review and meta-analysis. *Autism, 24*(8), 1933-1944.

John, R. P. S., Knott, F. J., & Harvey, K. N. (2018). Myths about autism: An exploratory study using focus groups. *Autism, 22*(7), 845-854. https://doi.org/10.1177/1362361317714990

Kimura, Y., Fujioka, T., Jung, M., Fujisawa, T. X., Tomoda, A., & Kosaka, H. (2020). An investigation of the effect of social reciprocity, social anxiety, and letter fluency on communicative behaviors in adults with autism spectrum disorder. *Psychiatry Research, 294*(113503). https://doi.org/10.1016/j.psychres.2020.113503

Kock, E., Strydom, A., Deirdre, O. B., & Tantam, D. (2019). Autistic women's experience of intimate relationships: the impact of an adult diagnosis. *Advances in Autism, 5*(1), 38-49. https://doi.org/10.1108/AIA-09-2018-0035

Lai, M.-C., & Baron-Cohen, S. (2015). Identifying the lost generation of adults with autism spectrum conditions. *The Lancet Psychiatry 2*(11), 1013-1027. https://doi.org/10.1016/S2215-0366(15)00277-1

Lamport, D., & Zlomke, K. R. (2014). The broader autism phenotype, social interaction anxiety, and loneliness: Implications for social functioning. *Current Psychology : A*

Journal for Diverse Perspectives on Diverse Psychological Issues, 33(3), 246-255.

Lau, W., & Peterson, C. C. (2011). Adults and children with Asperger syndrome: Exploring adult attachment style, marital satisfaction and satisfaction with parenthood. *Research in Autism Spectrum Disorders, 5*(1), 392-399.

Lawson, J., Baron-Cohen, S., & Wheelwright, S. (2004). Empathising and systemising in adults with and without Asperger Syndrome. *Journal of Autism and Developmental Disorders, 34*(3), 301-310.

Lewis, L. F. (2017). "We will never be normal": The experience of discovering a partner has autism spectrum disorder. *Journal of Marital and Family Therapy.*

Lipinski, S., Boegl, K., Blanke, E. S., Suenkel, U., & Dziobek, I. (2021). A blind spot in mental healthcare? Psychotherapists lack education and expertise for the support of adults on the autism spectrum. *Autism, 26*(6), 1509-1521. https://doi.org/10.1177/13623613211057973

Lorant, J. B. (2011). *Impact on emotional connectivity in couples in which one partner has Asperger's Syndrome* Alliant International University. WorldCat.org. https://www.proquest.com/dissertations-theses/impact-on-emotional-connectivity-couples-which/docview/880566433/se-2

Lowenstein, L. F. (2012). Learned Helplessness: The psychological condition of learned helplessness. *CRIMINAL LAW AND JUSTICE WEEKLY, 176*(9), 122-124.

Maenner, M. J., Shaw, K. A., Baio, J., Washington, A., Patrick, M., DiRienzo, M., Christensen, D. L., Wiggins, L. D., Pettygrove, S., Andrews, J. G., Lopez, M., Hudson, A., Baroud, T., Schwenk, Y., White, T., Rosenberg, C. R., Lee, L. C., Harrington, R. A., Huston, M., . . . PhD. (2020). Prevalence

References

of autism spectrum disorder among children aged 8 years - Autism and developmental disabilities monitoring network, 11 sites, United States, 2016. *Morbidity and mortality weekly report. Surveillance summaries (Washington, D.C. : 2002), 69*(4), 1-12. https://doi.org/10.15585/mmwr.ss6904a1

Mandy, W. (2019). Social camouflaging in autism: Is it time to lose the mask? *Autism, 23*(8), 1879-1881. https://doi.org/10.1177/1362361319878559

Marica, S. A. (2018). The adult with autism spectrum disorder– between myth and reality. *Arhipelag XXI Press, 2018.*

Marshack, K. J. (2009). *Life with a partner or spouse with Asperger Syndrome: Going over the edge? Practical steps to saving you and your relationship.* Autism Asperger Publishing Co.

Mendes, E. (2015). *Marriage and lasting relationships with Asperger's Syndrome (Autism Spectrum Disorder): Successful strategies for couples or counselors.* Jessica Kingsley Publishers.

Millar-Powell, N., & Warburton, W. A. (2020). Caregiver burden and relationship satisfaction in ASD-NT relationships. *Journal of Relationships Research, 11*(e15), 1-8. https://doi.org/10.1017/jrr.2020.11

Milley, A., & Machalicek, W. (2012). Decreasing students' reliance on adults: A strategic guide for teachers of students with Autism Spectrum Disorders. *Intervention in School and Clinic, 48*(2), 67-75. https://doi.org/10.1177/1053451212449739

Moreno, S. J., Wheeler, M., & Parkinson, K. (2012). *The partner's guide to Asperger Syndrome.* Jessica Kingsley.

Müller, E., Schuler, A., & Yates, G. B. (2008). Social challenges and supports from the perspective of individuals with Asperger syndrome and other autism spectrum disabilities. *Autism, 12*(2), 173-190. https://doi.org/10.1177/1362361307086664

Nadig, A., Lee, I., Singh, L., Bosshart, K., & Ozonoff, S. (2010). How does the topic of conversation affect verbal exchange and eye gaze? A comparison between typical development and high-functioning autism. *Neuropsychologia, 48*(9), 2730-2739. https://doi.org/10.1016/j.neuropsychologia.2010.05.020

Novacek, D. M., Gooding, D. C., & Pflum, M. J. (2016). Hedonic capacity in the broader autism phenotype: Should social anhedonia be considered a characteristic feature? *Frontiers in psychology, 7*(666), 1-8. https://doi.org/10.3389/fpsyg.2016.00666

O'Hearn, K., & Lynn, A. (2023). Age differences and brain maturation provide insight into heterogeneous results in autism spectrum disorder. *Frontiers in human neuroscience, 16*, 957375.

Pasch, L. A., Bradbury, T. N., & Davila, J. (1997). Gender, negative affectivity, and observed social support behavior in marital interaction. *Personal Relationships, 4*(4), 361-378.

Peachey, M., & Crane, L. (2024). "I don't understand their sense of belonging": Exploring how nonbinary autistic adults experience gender. *Autism in Adulthood, 6*(4), 462-473. https://doi.org/10.1089/aut.2023.0071

Pearson, A., & Rose, K. (2021). A conceptual analysis of autistic masking: Understanding the narrative of stigma and the illusion of choice. *Autism in Adulthood, 3*(1), 1-9. http://doi.org/10.1089/aut.2020.0043

Pellicano, E., Dinsmore, A., & Charman, T. (2014). What should autism research focus upon? Community views and priorities from the United Kingdom. *Autism, 18*(7), 756-770. https://doi.org/10.1177/1362361314529627

Pelzl, M. A., Travers-Podmaniczky, G., Brück, C., Jacob, H., Hoffmann, J., Martinelli, A., Hölz, L., Wabersich-Flad, D., & Wildgruber, D. (2022). Reduced impact of nonverbal

References

cues during integration of verbal and nonverbal emotional information in adults with high-functioning autism. *Front Psychiatry, 13*, 1069028. https://doi.org/10.3389/fpsyt.2022.1069028

Perkins, E. A., & Berkman, K. A. (2012). Into the unknown: Aging with autism spectrum disorders. *American Journal on Intellectual and Developmental Disabilities, 117*(6), 478-496. https://doi.org/10.1097/PAF.0b013e3181e5e0e2

Rench, C. (2014). *When eros meets autos: Marriage to someone with autism spectrum disorder* Doctoral dissertation, Capella University

ProQuest Dissertations Publishing. https://www.proquest.com/dissertations-theses/when-i-eros-meets-autos-marriage-someone-with/docview/1656449694/se-2

Robertson, A. E., Stanfield, A. C., Watt, J., Barry, F., Day, M., Cormack, M., & Melville, C. (2018). The experience and impact of anxiety in autistic adults: A thematic analysis. *Research in Autism Spectrum Disorders, 46*, 8-18. https://doi.org/10.1016/j.rasd.2017.11.006

Rossetti, J. (2020). *Relationship counselling with neurodiverse couples: "A long way to go".*

Sachdeva, N., & Jones, G. (2018). Diagnosis of autism in adulthood: What can we learn? *Good autism practice, 19*(2), 63-74.

Sato, W., Kochiyama, T., Uono, S., Yoshimura, S., Kubota, Y., Sawada, R., Sakihama, M., & Toichi, M. (2017). Reduced gray matter volume in the social brain network in adults with Autism Spectrum Disorder. *Frontiers in human neuroscience, 11*(395), 1-12. https://doi.org/10.3389/fnhum.2017.00395

Simone, R. (2009). *22 things a woman must know if she loves a man with Asperger's Syndrome.* Jessica Kingsley Publishers.

Smith, G. (2008). Does gender influence online survey participation?: A record-linkage analysis of university faculty online survey response behavior. *ERIC Document Reproduction Service No. ED 501717.*

Smith, R., Netto, J., Gribble, N. C., & Falkmer, M. (2020). 'At the end of the day, it's love': An exploration of relationships in neurodiverse couples. *Journal of Autism and Developmental Disorders, 51,* 3311-3321. https://doi.org/10.1007/s10803-020-04790-z

Sternberg, R. J., & Williams, W. M. (2010). *Educational psychology* (Second ed.). Pearson Education, Inc.

Swerdan, M. G., & Rosales, R. o. (2017). Comparison of prompting techniques to teach children with autism to ask questions in the context of a conversation. *Focus on Autism and Other Developmental Disabilities, 32*(2), 93-101.

Tantam, D., Kock, E., Strydom, A., & Deirdre, O. B. (2019). Autistic women's experience of intimate relationships: the impact of an adult diagnosis. *Advances in Autism, 5*(1), 38-49. https://doi.org/10.1108/AIA-09-2018-0035

Tobin, M. C., Drager, K. D. R., & Richardson, L. F. (2014). A systematic review of social participation for adults with autism spectrum disorders: Support, social functioning, and quality of life. *Research in Autism Spectrum Disorders, 8*(3), 214-229. https://doi.org/http://dx.doi.org/10.1016/j.rasd.2013.12.002

Van Der Miesen, A. I. R., Hurley, H., & De Vries, A. L. C. (2016). Gender dysphoria and autism spectrum disorder: A narrative review. *International review of psychiatry, 28*(1), 70-80. https://doi.org/10.3109/09540261.2015.1111199

References

Webster, G. D., Brunell, A. B., & Pilkington, C. J. (2009). Individual differences in men's and women's warmth and disclosure differentially moderate couples' reciprocity in conversational disclosure. *Personality and Individual Differences*, 46(3), 292-297. https://doi.org/https://doi.org/10.1016/j.paid.2008.10.014

White, S. W., Scarpa, A., Conner, C. M., Maddox, B. B., & Bonete, S. (2015). Evaluating change in social skills in high-functioning adults with autism spectrum disorder using a laboratory-based observational measure. *Focus on Autism and Other Developmental Disabilities*, 30(1), 3-12. https://doi.org/doi:10.1177/1088357614539836

Yew, R. Y., Hooley, M., & Stokes, M. A. (2023). Factors of relationship satisfaction for autistic and non-autistic partners in long-term relationships. *Autism*, 13623613231160244. https://doi.org/10.1177/13623613231160244

Yew, R. Y., Samuel, P., Hooley, M., Mesibov, G. B., & Stokes, M. A. (2021). A systematic review of romantic relationship initiation and maintenance factors in autism. *Personal Relationships*. https://doi.org/10.1111/pere.12397

Zamzow, R. M., Ferguson, B. J., Stichter, J. P., Porges, E. C., Ragsdale, A. S., Lewis, M. L., & Beversdorf, D. Q. (2016). Effects of propranolol on conversational reciprocity in autism spectrum disorder: A pilot, double-blind, single-dose psychopharmacological challenge study. *Psychopharmacology*, 233(7), 1171-1178. https://doi.org/10.1007/s00213-015-4199-0

Notes

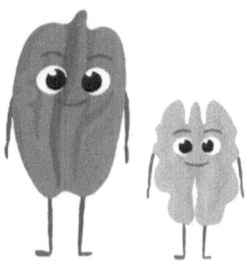

www.ingramcontent.com/pod-product-compliance
Lightning Source LLC
Chambersburg PA
CBHW030312080526
44584CB00012B/537